Prayers of a Daughter of the King

Finding Strength, Healing, and Identity in God's Presence

A 31-Day Devotional Prayer Journey for Women

Dr. Lende Click

Prayers of a Daughter of the King
Finding Strength, Healing, and Identity in God's Presence

Copyright © 2026 by **Lende Click**

All rights reserved.

No part of this book may be reproduced, stored in a retrieval system, or transmitted in any form or by any means—electronic, mechanical, photocopying, recording, or otherwise—without prior written permission from the author, except for brief quotations used in reviews.

Scripture quotations are taken from the **King James Version (KJV)** of the Bible.

This book is for inspirational and devotional purposes only.

Published by **Lende Click Publishing**

Author: Dr. **Lende Click**
Cover Design: Dr. **Lende Click**
Interior Design: Dr. **Lende Click**

Printed in the United States of America

Dedication

To every woman who has walked through pain, shed tears in silence, waited on God in the dark, and still chose to believe in His love.

This book is lovingly dedicated to you.

May these pages remind you that you are seen by God, held by His grace, healed by His presence, and deeply loved by your Heavenly Father.

No matter what you have faced, no matter what you are carrying, and no matter how weary your heart may feel, you are not forgotten.

You are chosen.
You are treasured.
You are a daughter of the King.

With love and prayer,

Dr. Lende Click

Table of Contents

Table of Contents

Introduction

Welcome, dear sister.

I am so thankful you are here.

Prayers of a Daughter of the King was written for women who desire to draw closer to God, to find healing in His presence, and to remember who they are in Him. This is a 31-day journey of prayer, Scripture, reflection, and quiet time with the Lord.

Life can be full of many things. There can be joy, but there can also be pain. There can be faith, but there can also be fear. There can be hope, but there can also be waiting, weariness, and questions. Many women carry silent burdens in their hearts. Some carry wounds from rejection, betrayal, grief, fear, or shame. Some are longing for peace, strength, direction, and a deeper sense of God's love.

This book was written as a gentle place to meet with God in the middle of all of that.

These pages are here to remind you that: you are chosen, you are deeply loved, you are not forgotten, you are not alone, and you are a daughter of the King.

Each day is meant to help you slow down and spend time in God's presence. As you read the devotionals, pray the prayers, reflect on the questions, and write in the journal prompts, my prayer is that your heart will be strengthened, healed, and drawn closer to the Lord.

You do not have to read this book perfectly. You do not have to rush. Take one day at a time. Let the words settle gently into your heart. Let the Scriptures speak about life to your soul. Let the prayers become a doorway into deeper fellowship with your Heavenly Father.

This journey is not about becoming perfect. It is about drawing near to the One who loves you perfectly.

Wherever you are in your walk with God today, I pray you will find peace in these pages. I pray you will be reminded of your worth in Christ. I pray you will feel the tenderness of God meeting you in your deepest needs. And I pray that as you go through these 31 days, your heart will rise stronger in faith, deeper in healing, and more secure in your identity as His beloved daughter.

May this book be a place of comfort, strength, renewal, and truth for you.

Welcome to this journey, dear sister.

You are a daughter of the King.

Day 1 — Chosen by the King

Key Scripture

"Ye have not chosen me, but I have chosen you..." — John 15:16

Devotional

Before you ever called on God, He had already set His love upon you.

Before you knew your purpose, before you understood your worth, before you found your way through the pain, the waiting, or the questions of life, God chose you. You are not an accident. You are not forgotten. You are not overlooked. You are not too broken, too weak, or too far behind for His love.

The King of kings looked upon your life with intention.

He chose you to be His daughter. He chose you to walk with Him. He chose you to grow in grace. He chose you to carry His peace, His beauty, and His light into a world that desperately needs Him.

Sometimes life can make a woman feel unwanted, unseen, or unworthy. Rejection, betrayal, comparison, failure, and disappointment can all try to whisper the lie that she does not matter. But the truth of God speaks louder than every wound and every lie.

You are chosen.

Not because you earned it.
Not because you are perfect.

Not because people always understood your heart.
But because God is gracious, loving, and faithful.

To be chosen by the King means your identity is no longer in what others said about you. Your identity is no longer in your past, your mistakes, your pain, or your fears. Your identity is in the One who formed you, called you, and loves you with an everlasting love.

Today, let your heart rest in this truth:
You belong to God.
You are loved by God.
You are chosen by the King.

Prayer

Heavenly Father,

Thank You for choosing me. Thank You that before I ever understood who I was, You already knew me, loved me, and called me Your own. When I feel forgotten, remind me that I am seen by You. When I feel rejected, remind me that I am accepted in Christ. When I feel weak, remind me that Your strength is made perfect in my weakness.

Help me not to find my worth in people's opinions, in past wounds, or in my own fears. Teach me to rest in Your love and to believe what Your Word says about me. I am not an accident. I am not abandoned. I am not without purpose. I am Your daughter.

Today I receive Your love. Today I embrace my identity in You. Today I choose to believe that I am chosen by the King.

In Jesus' name,
Amen.

Reflection Questions

1. Have there been times in your life when you felt unwanted, unseen, or overlooked?
2. What does it mean to you personally that God chose you?
3. What lies have you believed about your worth that God wants to replace with truth?
4. How can you walk today with the confidence of being God's daughter?

Declaration

I am chosen by the King.
I am loved, seen, and called by God.
My worth is not in the world's opinion of me.
My identity is in Christ.
I am a daughter of the King.

Journal Prompt

Write about a time when you felt rejected or unseen. Then write the truth God wants you to remember today: **I am chosen by the King.**

____

____

____

____

____

Day 2 — Deeply Loved

Key Scripture

"I have loved thee with an everlasting love: therefore with lovingkindness have I drawn thee." — Jeremiah 31:3

Devotional

There is nothing more healing to the heart than to know it is truly loved.

Many women carry silent questions deep inside:
Am I enough?
Am I wanted?
Am I worthy of love?
Will I always have to earn acceptance?

These questions often come from wounds, disappointments, rejection, or seasons when love felt distant, broken, or uncertain. Human love can be beautiful, but it can also be fragile. People may fail, leave, misunderstand, or disappoint. But God's love is not like that.

His love does not change with your emotions.
His love does not weaken when you struggle.
His love does not leave when you fail.
His love does not fade when life becomes hard.

God's love is everlasting.

Before you had the right words to pray, He loved you. Before you knew how to trust Him, He loved you. Before you found healing, before you overcame your fears, before you learned how to stand strong, His heart was already turned toward you.

You do not have to strive for His love. You do not have to perform for it. You do not have to prove that you deserve it. His love is a gift of grace. It is steady, faithful, tender, and true.

To be deeply loved by God means you are never alone in your sorrow, never forgotten in your waiting, and never abandoned in your weakness. His love reaches into the broken places and gently restores what pain tried to steal. His love covers you when you feel vulnerable. His love lifts you when your soul is tired.

Today, let yourself receive this truth:
You are deeply loved by God.
Not with a temporary love.
Not with a hesitant love.
But with an everlasting love.

Let His love quiet your fears. Let His love heals your heart. Let His love reminds you that you are precious in His sight.

You are deeply loved.

Prayer

Heavenly Father,

Thank You for loving me with an everlasting love. Thank You that Your love is not fragile, changing, or uncertain. Thank You that even in my weakness, You love me fully. Even in my tears, You stay near. Even in my questions, You remain faithful.

Lord, heal the places in my heart that have doubted love. Heal the wounds left by rejection, disappointment, or loss. Remove every lie that tells me I am not enough, not wanted, or not worthy. Fill those broken places with the truth of Your love.

Help me to stop striving for what You have already freely given. Teach me to rest in Your love and to believe that I am precious to You. Let Your love cast out fear, bring peace to my heart, and remind me that I am held securely in Your hands.

Today I receive Your love. Today I choose to believe Your Word. Today I rest in the truth that I am deeply loved.

In Jesus' name,
Amen.

Reflection Questions

1. Have you ever struggled to believe that you are truly loved?
2. What experiences in life may have made it hard for you to receive love?
3. How is God's love different from human love?
4. What would change in your heart if you truly rested in God's everlasting love?

Declaration

I am deeply loved by God.
His love for me is everlasting, faithful, and true.
I do not have to earn His love.
I am precious in His sight.
I rest in the love of my Heavenly Father.

Journal Prompt

Write a letter beginning with these words:
**"Father, thank You for loving me even
when..."** Then let your heart be honest before
God.

____

____

____

____

____

Day 3 — Fearfully and Wonderfully Made

Key Scripture

"I will praise thee; for I am fearfully and wonderfully made: marvellous are thy works; and that my soul knoweth right well." — Psalm 139:14

Devotional

So many women live under the heavy weight of comparison.

They compare their appearance, their gifts, their voice, their story, their success, their family, their journey, and even their faith. Comparison whispers that they are not enough. It tries to steal joy, confidence, and peace. It makes them focus on what they think they lack instead of seeing the beauty of how God created them.

But God did not make a mistake when He made you.

You were formed by His hands with care, purpose, and intention. Your life was not randomly put together. Your features, your personality, your gifts, your tenderness, your strength, and even the story He is writing through your life all matter to Him.

When the Bible says you are **fearfully and wonderfully made**, it means you were created with reverence, beauty, and divine purpose. You are the workmanship of God. There is something sacred in that truth. The King of heaven designed you.

The world may pressure you to look like someone else, act like someone else, or become someone else. But peace comes when you stop trying to be who you were never called to be and begin thanking God for who He created you to be.

You do not need to compete for worth.
You do not need to measure yourself against others.
You do not need to carry shame for how you look, where you come from, or what your journey has been.

You are God's creation.
You are His handiwork.
You are His daughter.

Even the parts of your story that feel weak or tender are not beyond His purpose. God can use every part of your life for His glory. What you thought was too small, too broken, or too ordinary can become part of the beauty of His plan.

Today, lift your eyes away from comparison and back to your Creator.

He made you with wisdom.
He made you with love.
He made you with purpose.

You are not less than.
You are not overlooked.
You are not a mistake.

You are fearfully and wonderfully made.

Prayer

Heavenly Father,

Thank You for creating me with purpose, beauty, and care. Thank You that I am fearfully and wonderfully made. Forgive me for the times I have compared myself to others and forgotten the value You placed on my life. Forgive me for speaking against myself, doubting my worth, or believing lies about who I am.

Lord, heal every place in me that carries insecurity, shame, or self-rejection. Teach me to see myself through Your eyes. Help me to honor the way You created me and to walk in confidence, not because of the world's approval, but because I belong to You.

Remind me that I do not have to be like anyone else to have value. Help me to rejoice in the person You created me to be. Let my heart rest in Your design, Your love, and Your purpose for my life.

Today I choose to reject comparison. Today I choose to embrace the truth that I am Your workmanship. Today I declare that I am fearfully and wonderfully made.

In Jesus' name,
Amen.

Reflection Questions

1. In what ways have you struggled with comparison?
2. Have you ever felt dissatisfied with how God made you?
3. What does it mean to you that you are fearfully and wonderfully made?
4. How can you begin to see yourself more through God's eyes and less through the world's standards?

Declaration

I am fearfully and wonderfully made.
God did not make a mistake when He made me.
I reject comparison and receive my God-given worth.
I am created with purpose, beauty, and
love. I am a daughter of the King.

Journal Prompt

Write down three things about yourself that you have struggled to accept.
Then beside each one, write this truth:
"God made me with purpose, and I will thank Him for His design."

Day 4 — Accepted in His Presence

Key Scripture

"To the praise of the glory of his grace, wherein he hath made us accepted in the beloved." — Ephesians 1:6

Devotional

Many women know what it feels like to want acceptance.

They want to be accepted by family, friends, church, or people around them. They want to feel included, valued, and loved. Sometimes they try very hard to please others so they will not feel left out or rejected.

But people's acceptance can change.

Some people accept you only when you agree with them.
Some accept you only when you are strong.
Some accept you only when you meet their expectations.

But God's acceptance is not like that.

When you come to Him through Jesus Christ, you are accepted in His presence. You do not have to fight for a place in His heart. You do not have to prove that you are good enough. You do not have to wear a mask and pretend that everything is fine.

God already knows everything about you.

He knows your past.
He knows your pain.
He knows your fears.
He knows your weaknesses.
And still, He welcomes you.

That is the beauty of His grace.

So many people carry the pain of rejection. Maybe someone did not love you well. Maybe someone walked away. Maybe someone made you feel unimportant. Maybe someone's words made you question your value. Those wounds can go deep.

But rejection from people does not remove your acceptance with God.

In His presence, you are welcomed.
In His presence, you are seen.
In His presence, you are
loved. In His presence, you
belong.

You do not have to earn the right to come near to Him. Jesus made the way for you. Because of His love and sacrifice, you can come boldly to the Father.

Today, let your heart rest in this truth:
You are accepted in the Beloved.
You are not too broken to come near.
You are not too wounded to be loved.
You are not too imperfect to be welcomed.

God is not asking you to come perfect.
He is asking you to come as you are.

And when you come into His presence, you will find grace, mercy, healing, and peace.

You are accepted in His presence.

Prayer

Heavenly Father,

Thank You for accepting me in Your presence. Thank You that I do not have to earn Your love or prove my worth to You. Thank You that through Jesus, I have a place near Your heart.

Lord, heal every wound of rejection in my life. Heal the pain of harsh words, broken relationships, and times when I felt unwanted or left out. Remove the lie that I do not belong. Remove the fear that I am not enough. Replace those lies with Your truth.

Help me to stop chasing the approval of people more than the peace of Your presence. Teach me to rest in the acceptance You have already given me in Christ. Remind me that I am welcomed, loved, and held by You.

Today I come to You just as I am. I bring You my weakness, my pain, my questions, and my heart. Thank You for receiving me with grace. Thank You for making me accepted in the Beloved.

In Jesus' name,
Amen.

Reflection Questions

1. Have you ever struggled with wanting acceptance from people?
2. Has rejection ever made you question your worth?
3. What does it mean to you that God accepts you in His presence?
4. How would your heart change if you truly rested in God's acceptance?

Declaration

I am accepted in the presence of God.
I do not have to earn His love.
Through Christ, I belong.
I am welcomed, loved, and seen by my Heavenly
Father. I am a daughter of the King.

Journal Prompt

Write about a time when you felt rejected or left out. Then write this truth over your heart today:
"In God's presence, I am fully accepted and deeply loved."

Day 5 — Called by Name

Key Scripture

"Fear not: for I have redeemed thee, I have called thee by thy name; thou art mine." — Isaiah 43:1

Devotional

There is something very personal about being called by name.

Your name is not just a word. It speaks of being known. It speaks of being seen. It speaks of being remembered. In a world where many people feel overlooked, forgotten, or unnoticed, it is a comfort to know that God does not see you as just one face in a crowd.

He knows your name.

He knows your story.
He knows your tears.
He knows your prayers.
He knows your struggles.
He knows the silent battles you do not talk about with anyone else.

God is not distant from your life. He is personal. He sees you fully and loves you deeply.

Sometimes women feel invisible. They serve, they care, they give, they carry burdens, and yet inside they may wonder, **Does anyone really see me? Does anyone understand what I carry? Does anyone know how much I hurt?**

God does.

He is the God who calls His daughters by name. He does not confuse you with someone else. He does not forget where you are. He does not lose sight of you in your pain, your waiting, or your lonely places.

When God says, **"I have called thee by thy name; thou art mine,"** it is a message of love, closeness, and belonging. It means you are precious to Him. It means you are not abandoned. It means your life matters to the One who created you.

To be called by name also means you are called with purpose. God did not only save you to be near Him; He also calls you forward into the life He has for you. He calls you out of fear. He calls you out of shame. He calls you out of the lies of the past. He calls you into truth, healing, and hope.

Today, remember this:
God knows your name.
God knows your need.
God knows your heart.
God knows your future.

You do not have to shout to be noticed by Him.
You do not have to hide your tears from Him.
You do not have to wonder if He sees you.

He sees you.
He knows you.
He calls you by name.

And when the King calls you by name, it means you are deeply loved and you truly belong.

Prayer

Heavenly Father,

Thank You for knowing me personally and for calling me by name.
Thank You that I am not forgotten, overlooked, or unseen by You.
Thank You that You know my heart, my story, my pain, and my needs
better than anyone else.

Lord, in the places where I have felt invisible, remind me that You see
me. In the places where I have felt forgotten, remind me that You
remember me. In the places where I have felt alone, remind me that
You are near.

Help me to believe that I matter to You. Help me to rest in the truth
that I am Yours. Remove every lie that says I am unnoticed, unwanted,
or unimportant. Replace those lies with the peace of knowing that I am
fully known and deeply loved by You.

Thank You for calling me out of fear and into faith. Thank You for
calling me out of pain and into healing. Thank You for calling me out
of darkness and into Your marvelous light.

Today I choose to believe that You know me, love me, and call me by
name.

In Jesus' name, Amen.

Reflection Questions

1. Have you ever felt unseen or forgotten?
2. What does it mean to you that God knows your name?
3. Are there areas in your life where you need to remember that
   God sees you personally?

4. How can the truth that God calls you by name bring comfort to
   your heart today?

Declaration

**God knows my name.
I am seen, known, and loved by Him.
I am not forgotten or overlooked.
I belong to my Heavenly
Father. I am a daughter of the
King.**

Journal Prompt

Write about a time when you felt unseen or forgotten. Then write this truth over that memory:
"God knew my name, saw my pain, and never left me."

____

____

____

____

____

Day 6 — Crowned with Dignity

Key Scripture

"She openeth her mouth with wisdom; and in her tongue is the law of kindness."
— Proverbs 31:26

Devotional

Many women have walked through seasons that tried to strip away their dignity.

Harsh words, rejection, betrayal, abuse, shame, failure, or painful mistakes can leave deep marks on the heart. Sometimes life can make a woman feel small, broken, or unworthy. Sometimes the enemy tries to whisper that because of what happened to her, or because of what she has been through, she no longer has value.

But that is not the truth.

God does not look at you with shame.
God does not look at you with disgust.
God does not look at you as less than.

He looks at you with love.

As a daughter of the King, you are crowned with dignity. That means your worth is not taken away by what others did to you. It is not taken away by what people said about you. It is not taken away by your past, your struggles, or your scars.

Dignity is the quiet beauty of knowing who you are in God.

It is not pride.
It is not pretending.
It is not thinking you are better than others.

It is walking in the truth that you belong to God and that your life carries value because He made you and loves you.

A woman crowned with dignity does not have to beg for worth. She does not have to prove herself to everyone. She does not have to let shame speak louder than grace. She can walk gently, speak wisely, and live with quiet strength because she knows her identity is secure in God.

Even if your past was painful, God can restore your dignity.
Even if people tried to tear you down, God can lift your head.
Even if you have felt ashamed, God can cover you with grace.

What was broken is not beyond His healing.
What was wounded is not beyond His touch.
What was humbled in pain can still rise in His strength.

Today, remember this:
You are not defined by your worst moment.
You are not defined by what others said about you.
You are not defined by your wounds.

You are a daughter of the King.
You are loved by God.
You are crowned with dignity.

Walk today with your head lifted, not because life has always been easy, but because God has been faithful.

Prayer

Heavenly Father,

Thank You that my worth comes from You. Thank You that I am not defined by my past, by my pain, or by the opinions of others. Thank You that in You, I am loved, valued, and crowned with dignity.

Lord, heal every wound that has made me feel ashamed, broken, or less than. Heal the pain of harsh words, rejection, failure, and disappointment. Remove every lie that tells me I have no value. Replace those lies with Your truth.

Teach me to walk in quiet strength and grace. Help me to carry myself as a daughter of the King. Let my words be filled with wisdom and kindness. Let my heart rest in the dignity You have given me through Your love.

Today I surrender every shame, every wound, and every fear to You. Thank You for lifting my head and reminding me who I am. I choose to walk in the dignity of being Your daughter.

In Jesus' name,
Amen.

Reflection Questions

1. Have there been times in your life when you felt ashamed or unworthy?
2. What experiences may have affected your sense of dignity?
3. What does it mean to you to be crowned with dignity by God?
4. How can you walk today with quiet strength and grace?

Declaration

I am crowned with dignity.
My worth comes from God.
I am not defined by shame, pain, or my past.
I am loved, valued, and upheld by my Heavenly
Father. I am a daughter of the King.

Journal Prompt

Write about an area of your life where shame or pain tried to steal your sense of worth. Then write this truth over it:
"God has crowned me with dignity, and my worth is secure in Him."

____

____

____

____

____

Day 7 — Secure in the Father's Arms

Key Scripture

"The eternal God is thy refuge, and underneath are the everlasting arms..."
— Deuteronomy 33:27

Devotional

There are times in life when everything feels uncertain.

Sometimes the heart feels shaken by fear, loss, disappointment, or pain.
Sometimes a woman may look around and feel that nothing is steady. People change. Situations change. Plans change. Emotions rise and fall. In those moments, it is easy to feel unsafe inside.

But God offers something the world cannot give.

He offers refuge.

He offers His presence.

He offers the security of His everlasting arms.

To be secure in the Father's arms does not mean life will always be easy. It does not mean there will never be sorrow, pressure, or tears. But it does mean that in every season, you have a place of safety in Him.

God is not far away from your struggles. He is near to you in them. When your heart feels tired, He holds you. When your mind feels overwhelmed, He covers you with peace. When your soul feels weak, He becomes your strength.

There is deep comfort in knowing that the Father's arms never fail.

Human strength may fail.
Human promises may fail.
Human understanding may fail.
But God's arms are everlasting.

He does not grow tired of holding you.
He does not become impatient with your tears.
He does not turn away when you feel weak.

He remains.

Some women have never felt truly safe. Some have walked through deep hurt, rejection, betrayal, or fear. Some have had to be strong for so long that they do not know how to rest. But the Father invites you into something beautiful today: rest in His arms.

You do not have to carry every burden alone.
You do not have to live in constant fear.
You do not have to keep pretending that you are fine.

You are allowed to rest in God.

You are allowed to lean on Him.

You are allowed to be held by His love.

Today, let this truth sink deep into your heart:
The eternal God is your refuge.
Underneath you are His everlasting arms.
You are not falling without help.

You are not facing life alone.
You are held by the Father.

Even when you cannot see the way ahead, His arms are still beneath you. Even when your heart feels fragile, His strength is still around you. Even when life feels uncertain, His love remains steady.

You are secure in the Father's arms.

Prayer

Heavenly Father,

Thank You for being my refuge and my safe place. Thank You that underneath me are Your everlasting arms. Thank You that when life feels uncertain, I am still secure in You.

Lord, calm every fear in my heart. Quiet every anxious thought in my mind. Heal the places in me that feel unsafe, tired, or overwhelmed. Help me to stop carrying burdens that were never meant to be carried alone.

Teach me to rest in Your love. Teach me to trust Your arms around my life. When I feel weak, remind me that Your strength holds me. When I feel afraid, remind me that Your presence is my peace. When I feel like I may fall, remind me that I am held by You.

Today I choose to lean on You. Today I choose to rest in You. Today I choose to believe that I am secure in the Father's arms.

In Jesus' name,
Amen.

Reflection Questions

1. Have there been seasons in your life when you felt unsafe, afraid, or overwhelmed?
2. What does it mean to you that God is your refuge?
3. Are there burdens you have been carrying that you need to place in the Father's arms today?
4. How can you practice resting more in God's care?

Declaration

God is my refuge and safe place.
I am held by His everlasting arms.
I do not have to live in fear.
I can rest in the love and strength of my Heavenly
Father. I am a daughter of the King.

Journal Prompt

Write about an area of your life where you need to feel God's safety and peace. Then write this truth over it:
"I am secure in the Father's arms, and He will hold me through every season."

____

____

____

____

Day 8 — A Daughter, Not an Orphan

Key Scripture

"For ye have not received the spirit of bondage again to fear; but ye have received the Spirit of adoption, whereby we cry, Abba, Father." — Romans 8:15

Devotional

Many women live with an orphan heart and do not even realize it.

An orphan heart feels alone.
It feels unwanted.
It feels as if it has to struggle for love, protection, and belonging.
It fears being rejected, forgotten, or left behind.

Even women who love God can sometimes carry this kind of pain inside. Past wounds, rejection, abandonment, betrayal, or deep disappointment can leave the heart feeling as though it must survive on its own. It may look strong on the outside, but inside it still feels afraid to trust, afraid to rest, and afraid to believe it truly belongs.

But in Christ, you are not an orphan.

You are a daughter.

When God saved you, He did not only forgive your sins. He brought you into His family. He gave you a place in His heart. He gave you His name, His love, and His presence. You are not on the outside looking in. You are not trying to earn a place in His house. Through Jesus, you belong to the Father.

This is what adoption means in the heart of God.

You have been received.
You have been wanted.
You have been loved.
You have been brought near.

An orphan spirit says, **"I am on my own."**
But a daughter's heart says, **"My Father cares for me."**

An orphan spirit says, **"I have to fight for love."**
But a daughter's heart says, **"I am already loved."**

An orphan spirit says, **"I do not belong."**
But a daughter's heart says, **"I have a home in God."**

Sometimes healing comes when God gently shows you that you have
been living from fear instead of from belonging. He does not reveal
this to shame you. He reveals it so He can heal you. He wants to teach
your heart to live as a daughter, secure in His love.

Today, you do not have to think like an orphan anymore.
You do not have to live as though you are alone.
You do not have to carry the fear of being left behind.

Your Heavenly Father has claimed you.
He has adopted you.
He welcomes you near.

You can cry, **"Abba, Father,"** because you are His.

You are not abandoned.
You are not outside the family of God.
You are not forgotten.

You are a daughter, not an orphan.

Prayer

Heavenly Father,

Thank You that through Jesus, I am not an orphan. Thank You that You have adopted me as Your daughter and brought me into Your family. Thank You that I do not have to live alone, afraid, or rejected. Thank You that I belong to You.

Lord, heal every orphan place in my heart. Heal every wound from rejection, abandonment, betrayal, and loss. Heal the parts of me that still feel unwanted or afraid to trust. Remove the lies that tell me I am on my own. Remove the fear that tells me I do not belong.

Teach me to live as Your daughter. Help me to rest in Your love, trust in Your care, and believe that I have a home in You. Let my heart grow secure in the truth that You are my Father and I am Yours.

Today I renounce the spirit of fear and receive the spirit of adoption. Today I choose to believe that I am loved, received, and held by You. Today I declare that I am a daughter, not an orphan.

In Jesus' name,
Amen.

Reflection Questions

1. Have you ever struggled with feeling alone, unwanted, or as if you had to fight for love?
2. In what ways have you seen an orphan heart show up in your life?
3. What does it mean to you that God has adopted you as His daughter?
4. How would your life change if you fully believed that you belong to the Father?

Declaration

I am a daughter, not an orphan.
I belong to my Heavenly Father.
I do not have to live in fear or rejection.
I am loved, received, and adopted by
God. I am a daughter of the King.

Journal Prompt

Write about any area in your life where you have felt alone, rejected, or as if you had to fight for love. Then write this truth over your heart: **"I am not an orphan. I am a beloved daughter of God."**

____

____

____

____

Day 9 — Bringing Your Brokenness to God

Key Scripture

"The Lord is nigh unto them that are of a broken heart; and saveth such as be of a contrite spirit." — Psalm 34:18

Devotional

Brokenness is not something people usually want to talk about.

Many women try to hide it.
They smile when they are hurting.
They stay busy so they do not have to feel the pain.
They tell others they are fine, even when their heart is heavy.

Sometimes brokenness comes from rejection.
Sometimes it comes from betrayal.
Sometimes it comes from grief, disappointment, loss, or deep wounds from the past.
And sometimes the pain is so deep that it feels hard to even find the right words.

But God is not afraid of your brokenness.

He is not uncomfortable with your tears.
He is not impatient with your pain.
He does not turn away from the wounded places in your heart.

He comes near.

The Bible says that the Lord is near to the brokenhearted. That means when your heart feels shattered, God is not far away. He is close. He sees every tear. He hears every silent cry. He knows the parts of your story that still ache inside.

Many people feel they must clean themselves up before coming to God. They think they need to be stronger, calmer, or more put together first. But God is not asking you to come perfect. He is asking you to come honest.

Bring Him your tears.
Bring Him your questions.
Bring Him your disappointment.
Bring Him your sorrow.
Bring Him your broken heart.

You do not have to hide the pieces from Him.

God is the One who heals what is broken. He knows how to touch the wounded places with gentleness. He knows how to restore what pain has damaged. He knows how to bring peace where there has been sorrow and hope where there has been despair.

Sometimes healing does not happen all at once. Sometimes it is a journey. But every healing journey begins with this simple step: bringing your brokenness to God.

You are not weak because you are hurting.
You are not failing because you are grieving.
You are not forgotten because your heart still aches.

You are human, and you are deeply loved by God.

Today, you do not have to carry your brokenness alone.
You do not have to pretend that everything is fine.
You do not have to bury the pain one more day.

Bring it to the Father.

He is near.
He is gentle.
He is faithful.
He is able to hold every broken piece.

Prayer

Heavenly Father,

Thank You that You are near to the brokenhearted. Thank You that I do not have to hide my pain from You. Thank You that You see every tear, every wound, and every part of my heart that still hurts.

Lord, today I bring You my brokenness. I bring You the pain I have carried, the sorrow I have hidden, and the wounds I do not always know how to explain. I bring You the disappointments, the grief, the rejection, and the places where my heart feels weak and tired.

Please meet me in those broken places. Heal what has been wounded. Comfort what has been grieving. Restore what has been damaged by pain. Help me not to be afraid to come to You honestly. Teach me to trust Your heart and to believe that You are gentle with me.

Thank You that I do not have to carry this alone. Thank You that You are not far away. Thank You that You are close to me, even in my pain. Today I lay my broken heart before You and ask You to begin healing every piece.

In Jesus' name,
Amen.

Reflection Questions

1. What has been weighing heavily on your heart lately?
2. Are there broken places in your life that you have been trying to hide?
3. Why do you think it can be hard to bring your pain honestly to God?
4. What would it look like for you to trust God with your brokenness today?

Declaration

God is near to my broken heart.
I do not have to hide my pain from Him.
He sees me, loves me, and cares for me.
I can bring every broken piece to my Heavenly
Father. I am a daughter of the King.

Journal Prompt

Write honestly about the broken places in your heart right now. Then end your writing with these words:
"Father, I bring my brokenness to You, and I trust You to hold every piece."

____

____

____

____

____

Day 10 — Healing from Rejection

Key Scripture

"But the Lord hath taken me up." — Psalm 27:10

Devotional

Rejection can wound the heart very deeply.

Sometimes it comes through words.
Sometimes it comes through silence.
Sometimes it comes when someone leaves, turns away, forgets you, or makes you feel that you are not enough.

Rejection has a way of making a woman question her worth. It can whisper painful lies like:

I am not wanted.
I am not enough.
Something is wrong with me.
I will always be left behind.

These lies can stay in the heart for a long time if they are not brought into the light of God's truth. But rejection from people does not mean rejection from God.

People may fail you, but God does not.
People may misunderstand you, but God knows your heart.
People may leave, but God remains.

The pain of rejection is real, but it does not have the final word over your life.

Psalm 27:10 gives such tender hope: **"But the Lord hath taken me up."** What a beautiful promise. Even when human love fails, God receives you. Even when others do not value you rightly, God draws you near. Even when rejection leaves an ache in your heart, the Father lifts you into His love.

Healing from rejection begins when you stop agreeing with the lie that your worth depends on who accepted you or who turned away from you.

Your worth was never in their hands.
Your worth is in God.
You are wanted by Him.
You are seen by Him.
You are loved by Him.
You are received by Him.

That does not mean rejection does not hurt. It does. But it means rejection does not define you.

Sometimes the wounds of rejection can come from childhood.
Sometimes from family.
Sometimes from friendship.
Sometimes from church.
Sometimes from marriage.
Sometimes from moments you never fully healed from.

God sees every wound. He does not overlook the tears that rejection caused. He knows how those moments shaped your fears, your insecurity, and your struggle to trust. And still, He gently says, **Come to Me. Let Me heal what rejection wounded.**

You do not have to keep living as if one person's rejection decided your value.
The love of God speaks a better word.

Today, let Him heal the places where rejection left pain.
Let Him replace lies with truth.
Let Him remind you that you are not abandoned.
You are not unwanted.
You are not forgotten.

You are held by the Father, and He has taken you up.

Prayer

Heavenly Father,

Thank You that when people fail me, You remain faithful. Thank You that when rejection wounds my heart, You are near to heal me. Thank You that my worth is not based on who accepted me or who turned away from me. My worth is in You.

Lord, today I bring You every wound of rejection. I bring You the words, the memories, the silence, the leaving, and the pain that made me feel unwanted or not enough. You know every place in my heart that still aches because of rejection. Please touch those places with Your healing love.

Remove every lie that rejection planted in me. Remove the fear of being abandoned. Remove the belief that I am unworthy of love. Replace those lies with Your truth. Remind me that I am wanted by You, loved by You, and received by You.

Help me not to build my identity on what others did or did not do. Help me to build my life on Your love. Heal my heart, restore my peace, and teach me to rest in the acceptance of my Heavenly Father.

Today I choose to believe that rejection does not define me. Your love does.

In Jesus' name,
Amen.

Reflection Questions

1. Have there been times in your life when rejection deeply wounded you?
2. What lies has rejection tried to make you believe about yourself?
3. How does it change your heart to know that God receives you fully?
4. What area of rejection do you need to surrender to God for healing today?

Declaration

Rejection does not define me.
My worth is in God.
I am wanted, loved, and received by my Heavenly Father.
The Lord has taken me up.
I am a daughter of the King.

Journal Prompt

Write about a rejection that still hurts your heart. Then write this truth over that wound:

"Even when people failed me, the Lord took me up and held me in His love."

____

____

____

____

Day 11 — Healing from Betrayal

Key Scripture

"Casting all your care upon him; for he careth for you." — 1 Peter 5:7

Devotional

Betrayal cuts deep because it comes from someone you trusted.

It may come from a friend, a family member, a spouse, a leader, or someone you opened your heart to. Betrayal hurts because it breaks trust. It leaves questions, tears, disappointment, and sometimes deep confusion.

You may wonder:

How could they do this?
Why did this happen?
Was I not enough?
Will I ever trust again?

These kinds of wounds are not small. Betrayal can leave the heart feeling heavy, guarded, and deeply wounded. Sometimes it even affects the way a woman sees herself, others, and God. But even in that pain, God is still near.

He sees the wound betrayal left behind.
He sees the tears no one else noticed. He sees the pain you carry in silence.

And He cares.

The Bible says, **"Casting all your care upon him; for he careth for you."** This means you do not have to carry betrayal alone. You can bring the anger, the sorrow, the confusion, and the broken trust to God. He is not afraid of your pain. He is the safest place to bring it.

Betrayal may have hurt you deeply, but it does not have to harden your heart forever.

God can heal the place where trust was broken.
God can comfort the place where love was wounded.
God can strengthen the place where your heart feels weak.

Healing from betrayal does not always happen quickly. Sometimes it takes time to process what was lost. Sometimes it takes time to grieve what was broken. But God can walk with you through every step. He can help you release what you cannot carry and heal what you cannot fix on your own.

Betrayal may tempt you to believe that you must never trust again, never open your heart again, or never let anyone come close again. But God does not want your wound to become your identity. He wants to heal you, restore you, and guard your heart with His peace.

Today, you do not have to pretend that betrayal did not hurt.
You do not have to bury the pain.
You do not have to carry the care of it alone.

Bring it to the Father.

He cares for you.
He will not betray you.
He will not fail you.
He will not turn away from your pain.

You are safe in His hands, and He is able to heal the wounds betrayal left behind.

Prayer

Heavenly Father,

Thank You that I can bring every pain to You because You care for me. Thank You that when betrayal wounds my heart, You do not turn away. Thank You that You see every tear, every question, and every place where trust has been broken.

Lord, today I bring You the pain of betrayal. You know what was done, what was said, and what was lost. You know how deeply it hurt me. Please heal the wound that betrayal left in my heart. Heal the sorrow, the anger, the confusion, and the fear that came with it.

Help me not to carry this pain alone. Teach me to cast every care upon You. Protect my heart from becoming hard, bitter, or hopeless. Replace my heaviness with Your peace. Replace my fear with Your comfort. Replace my broken trust with deeper trust in You.

Thank You that You are faithful and that You will never betray me. Thank You that I am safe in Your hands. Today I place this hurt before You and ask You to begin healing every broken place.

In Jesus' name,
Amen.

Reflection Questions

1. Has betrayal left a wound in your heart that still needs healing?
2. What feelings has betrayal brought into your life?
3. Why do you think betrayal can be so hard to release?
4. What would it look like for you to cast this care upon God today?

Declaration

**I do not have to carry betrayal alone.
God cares for me and is near to my pain.
He is faithful, and He will never fail me.
He is healing the wounded places in my
heart. I am a daughter of the King.**

Journal Prompt

Write honestly about a betrayal that wounded your heart. Then write
this truth over that pain:
"Father, I cast this care upon You because You care for me."

Day 12 — Healing from Fear

Key Scripture

"For God hath not given us the spirit of fear; but of power, and of love, and of a sound mind." — 2 Timothy 1:7

Devotional

Fear can touch many parts of a woman's life.

Sometimes it is fear of the future.
Sometimes it is fear of failure.
Sometimes it is fear of loss, rejection, sickness, heartbreak, or not knowing what will happen next.

Fear has a way of making the heart feel heavy and the mind feel tired. It can steal peace, disturb sleep, and make even small things feel overwhelming. It can whisper lies like:

What if everything goes wrong?
What if I am not strong enough?
What if I cannot handle what is ahead?

Fear tries to make you feel alone and unsafe. It tries to make problems look bigger than God's promises. It tries to keep your mind trapped in worry instead of resting in the Lord.

But fear is not from God.

The Bible says, **"For God hath not given us the spirit of fear; but of power, and of love, and of a sound mind."** That means fear does not have the right to rule your heart. It may knock on the door, but it does not have to stay.

God gives you something different.

He gives you **power** to stand.
He gives you **love** to calm your heart.
He gives you a **sound mind** so fear does not have to control your thoughts.

Healing from fear does not always mean that all fearful feelings disappear at once. Sometimes healing comes little by little as you keep bringing your heart back to God. It comes as you pray instead of panic. It comes as you trust instead of imagine the worst. It comes as you remember that the Lord is with you.

Fear says, **"You are not safe."**
But God says, **"I am with thee."**

Fear says, **"You will fall apart."**
But God says, **"My grace is sufficient for thee."**

Fear says, **"You are alone."**
But God says, **"I will never leave thee, nor forsake thee."**

The enemy wants fear to sit on the throne of your thoughts. But that place belongs to God alone.

Today, you do not have to let fear lead your heart.
You can bring every anxious thought to the Father.
You can place every worry in His hands.
You can ask Him to fill your heart with peace again.

God is greater than what you fear.
God is stronger than what feels overwhelming.
God is near to you in every uncertain place.

You do not have to be ruled by fear.

You can be healed by truth, held by love, and strengthened by the presence of God.

Prayer

Heavenly Father,

Thank You that You have not given me a spirit of fear. Thank You that You are with me and that I do not have to face life alone. Thank You that when my heart feels anxious and my mind feels overwhelmed, I can come to You for peace.

Lord, today I bring You every fear in my heart. I bring You the worries I keep thinking about, the unknowns that trouble me, and the burdens that make me feel weak. You know every fear I carry, even the ones I do not say out loud.

Please heal me from fear. Calm my heart and quiet my thoughts. Replace anxiety with Your peace. Replace panic with trust. Replace heaviness with the comfort of Your presence. Help me to remember that fear does not come from You and that I do not have to let it control my life.

Fill me with Your power, Your love, and a sound mind. Teach me to trust You more than I trust my fears. Help me to stand on Your Word and believe that You are faithful in every situation.

Today I give my fears to You. Today I choose to trust You. Today I declare that my heart belongs to You, not to fear.

In Jesus' name,
Amen.

Reflection Questions

1. What fears have been weighing on your heart lately?
2. How has fear affected your thoughts, peace, or choices?
3. What does it mean to you that God has given you power, love, and a sound mind?
4. What fear do you need to place into God's hands today?

Declaration

Fear does not rule me.
God is with me, and He is greater than what I fear.
He has given me power, love, and a sound mind.
I will trust my Heavenly
Father. I am a daughter of
the King.

Journal Prompt

Write down the fears that have been troubling your heart. Then write this truth over each one:
"God has not given me a spirit of fear. I place this fear into His hands."

____

____

____

____

Day 13 — Healing from Shame

Key Scripture

"There is therefore now no condemnation to them which are in Christ Jesus..."
— Romans 8:1

Devotional

Shame is a heavy burden.

It does not just say, **"I did something wrong."** It whispers, **"Something is wrong with me."**

That is why shame can go so deep. It tries to attach itself to your identity. It tries to make you feel dirty, unworthy, broken, and far from God. It tells you to hide. It tells you to stay silent. It tells you that if people knew everything, they would turn away.

Sometimes shame comes from your own mistakes.
Sometimes it comes from what others did to you.
Sometimes it comes from words spoken over your life.
Sometimes it comes from painful memories that still make your heart ache.

But shame does not tell the truth about who you are in Christ.

The Word of God says, **"There is therefore now no condemnation to them which are in Christ Jesus."** That means if you belong to Jesus, shame no longer has the right to define you. The cross of Christ is greater than your past. The mercy of God is greater than your failure. The love of God is greater than the voice of shame.

Shame says, **"Hide."**
But God says, **"Come near."**

Shame says, **"You are too dirty."**
But God says, **"I have washed you."**

Shame says, **"You are disqualified."**
But God says, **"My grace is enough for you."**

The enemy loves shame because shame keeps women bowed down. It keeps them from lifting their eyes to God. It keeps them from receiving love, walking in freedom, and believing they still have purpose. But Jesus did not die for you to live buried under condemnation.

He came to bring forgiveness.
He came to bring healing.
He came to bring freedom.

Healing from shame begins when you bring it into the light of God's truth. You stop agreeing with the voice that says you are ruined. You begin agreeing with the voice of your Father, who says you are loved, redeemed, and made new in Christ.

This does not mean your pain was not real.
It does not mean your mistakes did not
matter. It means shame does not get the last
word.

God is able to heal the places where shame settled in your heart. He can wash away what has made you feel unclean. He can restore what shame tried to steal. He can remind you that your identity is not in your lowest moment, but in the finished work of Jesus.

Today, you do not have to hide in shame.
You do not have to carry condemnation one more day.
You do not have to believe the lie that you are beyond grace.

In Christ, there is mercy.
In Christ, there is cleansing.
In Christ, there is freedom.

You are not defined by shame.
You are defined by the love of God.

Prayer

Heavenly Father,

Thank You that in Christ there is no condemnation. Thank You that Your mercy is greater than my past, my pain, and every voice of shame. Thank You that I do not have to hide from You. I can come near because of Your grace.

Lord, today I bring You every place in my heart where shame has settled. I bring You the memories, the failures, the wounds, and the words that made me feel dirty, unworthy, or broken. You know every burden I have carried in silence. Please heal those places with Your love.

Wash me with Your truth. Remind me that I am forgiven, loved, and made new in Christ. Remove the lie that I am disqualified or beyond grace. Break every chain of condemnation from my life. Teach me to walk in the freedom You have given me.

Help me to stop agreeing with shame and start agreeing with Your Word. Lift my head again. Restore my peace. Let my heart rest in the truth that I belong to You and that Your love has the final word over my life.

Today I lay down shame and receive Your mercy. Today I choose to believe that I am loved, redeemed, and free in Christ.

In Jesus' name,
Amen.

Reflection Questions

1. Have there been areas in your life where shame has made you want to hide?
2. Has shame ever made you feel distant from God?
3. What is the difference between conviction from God and condemnation from shame?
4. What truth from God's Word do you need to speak over your heart today?

Declaration

I am not defined by shame.
In Christ, there is no condemnation over my life.
I am forgiven, loved, and made new by God's grace.
Shame does not have the final word over
me. I am a daughter of the King.

Journal Prompt

Write about an area where shame has tried to speak over your life. Then write this truth over it:
"In Christ, I am forgiven, loved, and free from condemnation."

____

____

____

____

Day 14 — Healing from Grief

Key Scripture

"Blessed are they that mourn: for they shall be comforted." — Matthew 5:4

Devotional

Grief is a very tender pain.

It can come after losing a loved one.
It can come after losing a relationship.
It can come after losing a dream, a season, a part of life you can never get back, or even the life you thought things would be.

Grief is not always loud. Sometimes it is quiet. Sometimes it hides behind a smile. Sometimes it comes in waves. One moment you may feel strong, and the next moment a memory, a song, a date, or a thought can bring tears again.

Grief has a way of touching the deepest parts of the heart.

It can leave you feeling empty.
It can leave you feeling tired.
It can leave you feeling like words are too small for what you carry

inside. But even in grief, God is near.

Jesus said, **"Blessed are they that mourn: for they shall be comforted."**

What a tender promise. God does not ignore mourning. He does not
rush you through sorrow. He does not tell you to pretend you are fine.
He offers comfort.

Comfort means His presence comes near in the pain.
Comfort means you are not left alone in your sorrow.
Comfort means God holds you gently while your heart is healing.

Sometimes women feel they must be strong all the time. They may
think they need to stop crying, move on quickly, or hide the depth of
their grief. But grief is not weakness. Grief is the heart responding to
loss. And God is kind with grieving hearts.

You do not have to be ashamed of your tears.
You do not have to explain every emotion.
You do not have to heal on someone else's timeline.

God knows what was lost.
He knows why it hurts.
He knows the emptiness that grief can leave behind.

Healing from grief does not mean you stop caring. It does not mean
you forget. It means God begins to pour comfort into the hurting
places. It means He helps you carry what feels too heavy. It means He
slowly restores hope where sorrow once felt overwhelming.

Some grief stays tender for a long time. But even then, God remains
faithful. He knows how to sit with you in the ache. He knows how to
bring peace little by little. He knows how to hold your heart when
memories make you cry.

Today, you do not have to hide your grief.
You do not have to be strong by yourself.
You do not have to carry sorrow alone.

Bring your mourning to God.

He is the Father of mercies.

He is the God of all comfort.

He is close to the brokenhearted.
And He will meet you with tenderness in your grief.

Prayer

Heavenly Father,

Thank You that You are near when my heart is grieving. Thank You that You do not turn away from my sorrow. Thank You that You see every tear and understand every pain that words cannot fully explain.

Lord, today I bring You my grief. You know what I have lost. You know what my heart misses. You know the sorrow that still rises in me, and You know how deeply it hurts. Please comfort me in the places that still ache.

Hold my heart gently, Father. When the grief feels heavy, be my strength. When the tears come, be my comfort. When the sadness feels deep, remind me that I am not alone. Help me not to rush my healing or hide my pain. Teach me to rest in Your love while You care for my heart.

Please pour peace into the empty places. Bring hope where sorrow has felt overwhelming. Stay close to me in every wave of grief. Thank You that You are faithful, patient, and full of mercy.

Today I place my sorrow in Your hands and ask You to comfort me with Your presence.

In Jesus' name,
Amen.

Reflection Questions

1. What loss or sorrow has brought grief into your heart?
2. How has grief affected your emotions, strength, or peace?
3. Have you felt pressure to hide your grief or move on too quickly?

4. What would it look like for you to let God comfort you in your mourning today?

Declaration

God is near to me in my grief.
I do not have to carry sorrow alone.
My Heavenly Father comforts me with tenderness and love.
He sees my tears and holds my
heart. I am a daughter of the
King.

Journal Prompt

Write about the grief your heart has been carrying. Be honest with God about what you miss, what hurts, and what feels heavy. Then write this truth over your heart:
"The Lord will comfort me, and I am not alone in my grief."

____

____

____

____

Day 15 — When Your Heart Feels Weary

Key Scripture

"Come unto me, all ye that labour and are heavy laden, and I will give you rest."
— Matthew 11:28

Devotional

There are times when the heart grows weary.

Sometimes it is not just the body that feels tired.
Sometimes the soul feels tired too.

A weary heart may come from carrying too much for too long.
It may come from stress, pain, grief, disappointment, waiting, or trying to stay strong through many battles.
Sometimes a woman keeps going because she feels she has to, even though inside she feels drained, overwhelmed, and worn down.

A weary heart can feel heavy.

It can make simple things feel hard.
It can make joy feel far away.
It can make the mind feel full and the spirit feel weak.

But Jesus speaks such a tender invitation:
"Come unto me... and I will give you rest."

He does not say, **"Come when you are stronger."**

He does not say, **"Come when you have everything together."**
He does not say, **"Come after you fix yourself."**
He simply says, **"Come."**

What a loving Savior.

When your heart feels weary, Jesus does not push you away. He calls you near. He knows that sometimes you are tired in places no one else can see. He knows the quiet burdens you carry. He knows the prayers you have prayed again and again. He knows the weight you have held in silence.

And He offers rest.

This rest is not only physical. It is rest for the soul. It is the deep peace of knowing you do not have to carry life by yourself. It is the comfort of laying your burdens at His feet. It is the strength that comes when His presence meets your weakness.

Sometimes women feel guilty for being weary. They think they should be stronger, more joyful, or able to handle everything better. But weariness is not failure. It is a sign that you need the Lord's refreshing.

God never asked you to be enough on your own. He asked you to come to Him.

You do not have to keep pretending you are fine.
You do not have to keep carrying every burden by yourself.
You do not have to keep running on empty.

Bring your weary heart to Jesus.

Let Him hold what feels too heavy.
Let Him quiet what feels anxious.
Let Him strengthen what feels weak.
Let Him give rest to the tired places in your soul.

Today, remember this:
Jesus sees your weariness.
Jesus understands your heaviness.
Jesus is not disappointed in your weakness. He is inviting you closer.

There is rest in His presence.
There is peace in His love.
There is strength for the weary heart in the arms of the Savior.

Prayer

Heavenly Father,

Thank You that I can come to You when my heart feels weary. Thank You
that You do not ask me to carry life alone. Thank You that in my
tiredness, weakness, and heaviness, You still welcome me near.

Lord, today I bring You my weary heart. You know the burdens I have
been carrying. You know the stress, the sorrow, the waiting, and the
pressure that have made my soul feel tired. Please meet me in those
weary places.

Give me rest, Father. Quiet the noise in my mind. Calm the heaviness
in my heart. Strengthen me where I feel weak. Refresh me where I feel
drained. Help me to stop striving in my own strength and to lean fully
on You.

Teach me to rest in Your presence without guilt. Remind me that I do
not have to be strong all the time because You are my strength. Thank
You that You are gentle with me and kind to my tired soul.

Today I lay my burdens at Your feet. Today I choose to come to You
for rest. Today I trust You to renew my heart.

In Jesus' name,
Amen.

Reflection Questions

1. What has been making your heart feel weary lately?
2. Have you been carrying burdens that feel too heavy for you?
3. Why is it sometimes hard to admit when your soul is tired?
4. What would it look like for you to truly rest in Jesus today?

Declaration

Jesus gives rest to my weary heart.
I do not have to carry every burden alone.
God is my strength when I feel weak.
I can come to Him just as I
am. I am a daughter of the
King.

Journal Prompt

Write honestly about what has been making your heart feel tired. Then write this truth over your soul today:
"Jesus sees my weariness, and He will give me rest."

____

____

____

____

Day 16 — Letting God Carry You

Key Scripture

"Cast thy burden upon the Lord, and he shall sustain thee..." — Psalm 55:22

Devotional

Many women are used to carrying a lot.

They carry responsibilities.
They carry pain.
They carry worries for their family.
They carry disappointments, memories, fears, and silent struggles that no one else sees.

Sometimes they carry so much for so long that they forget what it feels like to rest. They become used to holding everything together, staying strong, and pushing through. But deep inside, the heart can become tired, heavy, and overwhelmed.

God never meant for you to carry everything by yourself.

His Word says, **"Cast thy burden upon the Lord, and he shall sustain thee."** That is a loving invitation. God is telling you that what feels too heavy for your shoulders can be placed into His hands.

To let God carry you does not mean you stop caring.
It does not mean you give up.
It does not mean your responsibilities disappear.
It means you stop trying to hold every burden in your own strength.
It means you let God support you where you feel weak.

It means you trust Him with what you cannot control.
It means you stop carrying things in fear and start placing them into
the Father's hands.

Some burdens are too heavy for the human heart. Worry can wear you
down. Grief can drain you. Fear can make your mind restless. Pain can
make you feel like you are barely holding on. But the Lord is strong
enough to hold what is too much for you.

You do not have to carry tomorrow.
You do not have to carry everyone's outcome.
You do not have to carry every answer.
You do not have to carry every fear.
You can let God carry you.

Sometimes letting God carry you looks like praying instead of
panicking. Sometimes it looks like surrendering instead of striving.
Sometimes it looks like saying, **"Father, this is too heavy for me, but
it is not too heavy for You."**

That kind of surrender is not weakness. It is trust.

God is not asking you to be strong enough for everything. He is asking
you to lean on Him. His strength is made perfect in your weakness.
His hands are steady when your heart feels shaky. His peace can hold
you when life feels uncertain.

Today, you do not have to keep carrying what is crushing your heart.
You do not have to hold yourself together all alone.
You do not have to be afraid to place your burdens into God's hands.

He is able to sustain you.
He is able to strengthen you.
He is able to carry what you cannot.

You are safe in His care.
You are held in His love.
And you can let God carry you.

Prayer

Heavenly Father,

Thank You that I do not have to carry life alone. Thank You that when my burdens feel too heavy, I can place them into Your hands. Thank You that You are strong enough to hold what feels too much for me.

Lord, today I bring You every burden I have been carrying. I bring You my worries, my pain, my fears, my responsibilities, and the things that have made my heart feel heavy. You know what feels too hard for me right now. You know what has been wearing me down.

Please help me to release these burdens to You. Teach me to stop striving in my own strength and to trust Your care for me. Sustain me where I feel weak. Calm me where I feel anxious. Strengthen me where I feel tired. Hold me where I feel like I may fall.

Father, I confess that sometimes I try to carry things that only You can hold. Forgive me for the times I have trusted my own strength more than Your faithfulness. Today I surrender again. Today I choose to lean on You. Today I believe that You will sustain me.

Thank You for carrying me with love, patience, and mercy. Thank You that I am never alone under the weight of life. I place my burdens into Your hands and rest in Your care.

In Jesus' name, Amen.

Reflection Questions

1. What burdens have you been carrying that feel too heavy for your heart?
2. Why do you think it is sometimes hard to let God carry you?
3. Are there areas where you have been striving instead of surrendering?
4. What would it look like for you to place one burden into God's hands today?

Declaration

**I do not have to carry everything
alone. I can cast my burdens on the
Lord.
God will sustain me and strengthen me.
His hands are able to hold what is too heavy for
me. I am a daughter of the King.**

Journal Prompt

Write down the burdens that have been weighing on your heart. Then, one by one, write this truth after each one:
"Lord, I place this burden into Your hands, and I trust You to sustain me."

Day 17 — Trusting God in the Waiting

Key Scripture

"But they that wait upon the Lord shall renew their strength…" — Isaiah 40:31

Devotional

Waiting can be one of the hardest parts of faith.

It is not easy to wait when you are praying for answers.
It is not easy to wait when your heart is hoping for change.
It is not easy to wait when you do not understand why God has not moved yet.

Sometimes you may wait for healing.
Sometimes you may wait for direction.
Sometimes you may wait for restoration, provision, open doors, or peace in a difficult season.

Waiting can make the heart feel tired. It can bring questions like:
Lord, do You see me?
Lord, why is this taking so long?
Lord, are You still working?

But even in the waiting, God is faithful.

The Bible says, **"But they that wait upon the Lord shall renew their strength."** This means waiting is not wasted when it is placed in God's hands. Waiting is not just standing still with an empty heart. Waiting on the Lord is trusting Him, looking to Him, praying, and believing that He is still working even when you cannot see it yet.

God is never late.
God is never careless.
God is never absent in your waiting.

Sometimes while you are waiting for God to change your situation, He is also working in your heart. He is building trust, deepening faith, teaching surrender, and preparing you for what is ahead. The waiting season may feel quiet, but heaven is not silent. God is doing what you cannot yet see.

Waiting does not mean God has forgotten you.
Waiting does not mean your prayers were ignored.
Waiting does not mean nothing is happening.

It means you are being called to trust His timing.

That can be hard, especially when your heart is tired. But the beautiful promise is this: as you wait on the Lord, He renews your strength. He gives grace for the day you are in. He holds you steady when you want to give up. He reminds you that His plans are still good, even when the path feels slow.

You do not have to understand everything to trust Him.
You do not have to see the whole picture to believe He is faithful.
You do not have to force the answer before its time.

You can rest in this truth:
God is working in the waiting.
God is present in the waiting.
God is faithful in the waiting.

Today, if your heart feels tired from waiting, bring that weariness to the Father. Let Him renew your strength. Let Him steady your faith. Let Him remind you that delay is not the same as denial.

What He has promised, He is still able to do.

Prayer

Heavenly Father,

Thank You that You are faithful, even in seasons of waiting. Thank You that when I cannot see what You are doing, You are still working. Thank You that You do not forget me, overlook me, or leave me alone in the waiting.

Lord, You know the things I have been praying for. You know the answers I long for, the burdens I carry, and the places where my heart has grown tired. Waiting is not always easy for me. Sometimes I feel discouraged, confused, or weary. But today I choose to bring those feelings to You.

Please renew my strength, Father. Help me not to lose heart while I wait. Teach me to trust Your timing, even when I do not understand it. Calm my fears, quiet my questions, and steady my heart in Your love.

Help me to believe that You are working, even when I cannot see it. Help me to wait with faith, not with despair. Let this season draw me closer to You, not farther from You. Grow patience, trust, and hope in me while I wait.

Today I place my timeline into Your hands. Today I choose to trust Your heart. Today I believe that You are faithful in every waiting season.

In Jesus' name,
Amen.

Reflection Questions

1. What area of your life feels like a waiting season right now?
2. How has waiting affected your heart, thoughts, or faith?
3. Why do you think trusting God in the waiting can be difficult?

4. What does it mean to you that God renews your strength while you wait on Him?

Declaration

God is faithful in my waiting season.
He is working even when I cannot see it.
My waiting is not wasted in His hands.
He will renew my strength as I trust
Him. I am a daughter of the King.

Journal Prompt

Write about the area where you have been waiting on God. Be honest about what feels hard. Then write this truth over your heart:
"God is working in my waiting, and He will renew my strength."

____

____

____

____

____

Day 18 — Surrendering Your Plans

Key Scripture

"Trust in the Lord with all thine heart; and lean not unto thine own understanding. In all thy ways acknowledge him, and he shall direct thy paths."
— Proverbs 3:5–6

Devotional

It is natural to make plans.

We plan for our future.
We plan for our family.
We plan for our work, our hopes, and the things we dream about.

There is nothing wrong with making plans. But sometimes life does not go the way we expected. Doors close. Delays happen. Prayers are answered in a different way than we hoped. And when that happens, the heart can feel disappointed, confused, or even afraid.

That is when surrender becomes important.

Surrendering your plans to God does not mean you stop caring.
It does not mean your dreams do not matter.
It does not mean you should never hope for anything.

It means you trust God more than your own understanding.

The Bible says, **"Trust in the Lord with all thine heart; and lean not unto thine own understanding."** Sometimes we want to understand everything before we trust. We want to know why something changed, why something did not work out, or why the road ahead looks different than what we imagined. But faith does not always come with full explanation.

Sometimes faith says,
"Lord, this is not what I planned, but I still trust You."

That kind of surrender is not easy. It may come with tears. It may come with letting go of expectations. It may come with laying down what you wanted and choosing to believe that God's way is still good.

God sees what you cannot see.
He knows what you do not know.
He understands what is ahead before you ever arrive there.

What feels like a loss to you may be God's protection.
What feels like a delay may be His preparation.
What feels like a closed door may be His mercy leading you somewhere better.

Surrender is not giving up on God.
It is giving your plans to God.

It is saying,
"Father, I trust Your wisdom more than my own."
"I trust Your timing more than my own."
"I trust Your path more than the one I had in mind."

That kind of trust brings peace.

You do not have to control every outcome.
You do not have to force every answer.
You do not have to be afraid when your plans change.

The God who directs your path is faithful. He is not confused about your life. He is not surprised by what changed. He is not unsure of how to lead you. When you surrender your plans to Him, you are placing your future into loving and trustworthy hands.

Today, if your heart is struggling because things are not going as planned, bring that disappointment to God. Let Him meet you there. Let Him steady your heart. Let Him remind you that His plans are higher, wiser, and full of love.

You can trust Him with the road ahead.

Prayer

Heavenly Father,

Thank You that Your wisdom is greater than mine and Your plans are higher than my own. Thank You that even when I do not understand the road I am on, You still know exactly where You are leading me.

Lord, today I surrender my plans to You. I surrender my expectations, my timeline, my desires, and the things I thought would happen differently. You know the places where I feel disappointed, confused, or afraid because life has not gone the way I planned.

Help me to trust You with all my heart. Teach me not to lean on my own understanding. When I want answers, give me peace. When I want control, teach me surrender. When I feel uncertain, remind me that You are directing my path.

Father, I do not want to cling so tightly to my own plans that I miss the beauty of Your will. Help me to open my hands and trust Your heart. Give me grace to believe that even when things change, Your love remains the same and Your purpose for my life is still good.

Today I place my plans before You. Today I choose trust over fear. Today I believe that You will direct my path with wisdom, love, and faithfulness.

In Jesus' name,
Amen.

Reflection Questions

1. Is there an area of your life where things have not gone as you planned?
2. How do you usually respond when your plans change?
3. Why do you think surrender can be difficult?
4. What would it look like for you to trust God more than your own understanding today?

Declaration

I trust God more than my own understanding.
I surrender my plans into His hands.
He is wise, faithful, and good.
He will direct my path.
I am a daughter of the King.

Journal Prompt

Write about an area where your plans have changed or not worked out the way you hoped. Then write this truth over your heart:
"Lord, I surrender my plans to You and trust that Your path is best for me."

____

____

____

____

Day 19 — Walking by Faith, Not by Sight

Key Scripture

"For we walk by faith, not by sight."
— 2 Corinthians 5:7

Devotional

Walking by faith is not always easy.

It is much easier to feel strong when you can see the answer.
It is easier to have peace when you know exactly what is going to
happen. It is easier to trust when the road ahead looks clear.

But many times, faith does not work that way.

There are seasons when you cannot see the full picture.
There are moments when you do not know how God will provide.
There are times when you pray, wait, and still do not understand
what He is doing.

That is when faith becomes very real.

The Bible says, **"For we walk by faith, not by sight."** This means we
do not base our whole life on what we can see with our natural eyes.
We base our hearts on the truth of who God is. We trust His character
even when the path feels unclear.

Walking by sight says,
"I will trust when I can see everything."

Walking by faith says,
"I will trust because God is faithful, even when I cannot see everything."

Faith does not mean you ignore reality. It does not mean you pretend things are easy. It does not mean you never feel uncertain.

It means you choose to believe that God is still working beyond what your eyes can see.

Sometimes all you can see is the problem.
Sometimes all you can see is the delay.
Sometimes all you can see is the closed door, the unanswered prayer, or the difficult season.

But faith lifts your eyes higher.

Faith remembers that God is still on the throne.
Faith remembers that His promises are still true.
Faith remembers that what is impossible for you is not impossible for Him.

Walking by faith often means taking one step at a time. It means obeying God even when you do not know the whole plan. It means trusting His hand when you cannot trace His ways. It means believing that His love has not changed just because your circumstances feel uncertain.

A woman of faith does not have to have every answer.
She does not have to see the end from the beginning.
She simply has to keep walking with God.

Maybe today your path feels unclear.
Maybe you are in a place where you cannot see what God is doing.
Maybe you are asking questions and longing for direction.

Take heart.

You do not need to see everything to trust the One who does.

God sees the road ahead.
God knows the next step.
God understands what your eyes cannot yet see.

And if He is leading you, you can walk forward by faith.

Today, do not let what you see become bigger than what God has said.
Do not let uncertainty steal your
trust. Do not let fear lead your steps.

Walk by faith.
Trust His heart.
Follow His voice.
And believe that the God who called you will also carry you.

Prayer

Heavenly Father,

Thank You that I can trust You even when I do not see the full picture.
Thank You that Your faithfulness does not change, even when my
circumstances feel uncertain. Thank You that I do not have to
understand everything to walk with You.

Lord, today I confess that sometimes it is hard to trust when I cannot
see what You are doing. Sometimes I want answers, clarity, and proof
before I move forward. But today I choose faith over fear. I choose to
believe that You are working, even when I cannot see it.

Help me to walk by faith and not by sight. Strengthen my heart when
the path feels unclear. Steady my steps when I feel uncertain. Remind
me that Your promises are true and that Your hand is still upon my life.

Teach me to trust Your character more than my circumstances. Help me not to be ruled by what I see around me. Lift my eyes to You. Fill me with peace, courage, and confidence in Your love.

Today I place my unknowns into Your hands. Today I choose to follow You one step at a time. Today I believe that You are faithful, and I will walk by faith.

In Jesus' name,
Amen.

Reflection Questions

1. Is there an area of your life where you are struggling because you cannot see the outcome?
2. How do you usually respond when the path ahead feels unclear?
3. What does it mean to you personally to walk by faith and not by sight?
4. What is one step of faith God may be asking you to take today?

Declaration

I will walk by faith, not by sight.
God is faithful even when I cannot see the whole picture.
I trust His heart, His promises, and His leading.
He will guide me one step at a
time. I am a daughter of the
King.

Journal Prompt

Write about an area where you are having a hard time trusting because you cannot see the answer yet. Then write this truth over your heart: **"I do not have to see everything to trust the God who sees all things."**

Day 20 — Strength for the Battle

Key Scripture

"Be strong in the Lord, and in the power of his might." — Ephesians 6:10

Devotional

Life can feel like a battle sometimes.

There are battles in the mind.
There are battles in the heart.
There are battles in relationships.
There are battles with fear, discouragement, temptation, sorrow, and spiritual attack.

Some battles are seen.
Some are unseen.
But all of them can leave a woman feeling tired, weak, and worn down.

There are times when you may feel like you have fought for a long time. You may feel tired of praying, tired of standing, tired of carrying the burden, and tired of trying to stay strong. But God does not ask you to fight in your own strength.

His Word says, **"Be strong in the Lord, and in the power of his might."**

That means your strength does not have to come from yourself.
It comes from Him.

When you feel weak, He is strong.
When you feel empty, He can fill you.
When you feel like giving up, He can steady you and help you stand.

The enemy wants you to feel powerless. He wants you to believe that the battle is too big, that your prayers do not matter, and that you will never overcome. But that is not the truth. The God who is with you is greater than the battle before you.

You are not fighting alone.
You are not standing alone.
You are not praying alone.

The Lord is with you.

Strength for the battle does not always mean loud strength. Sometimes it looks quiet. Sometimes it looks like getting up and praying one more time. Sometimes it looks like choosing faith when fear is loud. Sometimes it looks like standing on God's Word even when emotions are shaking. Sometimes it looks like trusting God when you feel weak.

That is still strength.

A daughter of the King does not have to pretend she is never tired. But she can learn where true strength comes from. It comes from the presence of God. It comes from His Word. It comes from prayer. It comes from knowing that the battle belongs to the Lord.

Some battles will not be won by human effort alone. They must be fought in prayer, in surrender, and in trust. God knows how to strengthen your heart for what you are facing. He knows how to give courage to the weary soul. He knows how to help you stand when life feels heavy.

Today, if you feel like you are in a battle, do not lose heart.
Do not measure your strength only by how you
feel. Do not think you are alone because the fight is
hard.

Lift your eyes to the Lord.

He is your strength.
He is your defender.
He is your help.
He is your victory.

You may feel weak, but you are not without help.
You may feel tired, but God is still able to strengthen you.
You may be in a battle, but the Lord is still with you.

Be strong in the Lord.
He will give you strength for the battle.

Prayer

Heavenly Father,

Thank You that I do not have to fight my battles alone. Thank You that when I feel weak, Your strength is still available to me. Thank You that You are my help, my defender, and my refuge in every battle I face.

Lord, today I bring You the battles in my life. You know the struggles in my mind, my heart, my relationships, and the quiet places where I feel weary. You know what has been heavy, what has been painful, and what has made me feel tired inside.

Please strengthen me in You. Fill me with the power of Your might. When I feel weak, help me stand. When I feel afraid, give me courage. When I feel discouraged, remind me that You are with me and that the battle does not belong to me alone.

Teach me to fight in prayer, faith, and trust. Help me not to depend only on my own strength. Remind me that Your Word is truth, Your presence is near, and Your power is greater than every battle I face.

Today I choose to look to You for strength. Today I choose to believe that You will help me stand. Today I place every battle into Your hands and trust You to carry me through.

In Jesus' name,
Amen.

Reflection Questions

1. What battle are you facing in this season of your life?
2. In what ways has this battle left you feeling weak or tired?
3. What does it mean to you to be strong in the Lord instead of in yourself?
4. How can you lean more on God's strength today?

Declaration

I am strong in the Lord and in the power of His might.
I do not fight my battles alone.
God is my strength, my help, and my defender.
He will help me stand in every battle. I am a daughter of the King.

Journal Prompt

Write about the battle you are facing right now. Be honest about what feels heavy, hard, or tiring. Then write this truth over your heart: **"The Lord is my strength, and He will give me grace for this battle."**

Day 21 — Standing on God's Promises

Key Scripture

"For all the promises of God in him are yea, and in him Amen..." — 2 Corinthians 1:20

Devotional

There are times in life when everything feels uncertain.

Circumstances may change.
People may disappoint you.
Plans may not go the way you hoped.
Emotions may rise and fall from one day to the next.

In those moments, your heart needs something steady to stand on.

That is why God's promises are so precious.

His promises are not empty words.
They are not weak hopes.
They are not things that change with the weather or with your feelings.

God's promises are true because God is true.

When everything around you feels shaky, His Word remains firm.
When fear tries to speak, His promises speak louder. When your heart
is tired, His promises become strength for your soul.

Standing on God's promises means choosing to believe His Word even when your emotions feel weak. It means holding on to what God has said, even when the answer has not come yet. It means reminding your heart that God is faithful and that He will do what He says.

Sometimes the battle is not only around you. Sometimes it is in your thoughts. Fear, doubt, and discouragement may try to make you question whether God will really come through. But this is where faith becomes strong. Faith says:

God is still faithful.
His Word is still true.
His promises still stand.

Maybe today you need His promise of peace.
Maybe you need His promise of strength.
Maybe you need His promise of provision, comfort, wisdom, or His presence.

Whatever you need, His heart is faithful.

Standing on God's promises does not mean you will never have questions. It means your questions will not have the final word. God's truth will. His promises become the ground beneath your feet when life feels uncertain.

A daughter of the King does not stand only on what she sees.
She stands on what God has said.

When the enemy whispers lies, stand on the promise that God is with you. When fear says you will not make it, stand on the promise that His grace is sufficient.

When your heart feels troubled, stand on the promise that He will never leave you nor forsake you.

The promises of God are not fragile.
They are strong.

They are sure.
They are anchored in His faithful character.

Today, if your heart feels shaky, go back to His Word. Let His promises hold you. Let them strengthen your faith and quiet your fears. Let them remind you that God has not changed.

You can stand on His promises because He never fails.

Prayer

Heavenly Father,

Thank You for Your precious promises. Thank You that Your Word is true, steady, and faithful. Thank You that when life feels uncertain, I can stand on what You have said.

Lord, today I ask You to strengthen my heart through Your promises. When fear comes, remind me of Your truth. When doubt tries to speak, help me remember that You are faithful. When my emotions feel weak, help me stand on Your Word instead of my feelings.

Teach me to trust what You have spoken. Help me not to be moved by every situation around me. Let Your promises become strength in my weakness, peace in my anxiety, and hope in my waiting.

Father, thank You that every promise You have given is anchored in Your love and faithfulness. Help me to hold tightly to Your Word and to believe that You will do what You have said. Even when I do not see the answer yet, I choose to trust You.

Today I stand on Your promises. Today I place my faith in Your truth. Today I believe that You are faithful and Your Word will not fail me.

In Jesus' name,
Amen.

Reflection Questions

1. What promise from God do you need to hold onto in this season?
2. When life feels uncertain, what do you usually stand on?
3. How can God's promises bring strength and peace to your heart today?
4. What would change if you trusted God's Word more than your fears?

Declaration

I stand on the promises of God.
His Word is true, steady, and faithful.
I will not be ruled by fear or doubt.
God will do what He has
said.
I am a daughter of the
King.

Journal Prompt

Write about an area in your life where you need to stand on God's promises. Then write this truth over your heart:
"God is faithful, and His promises will hold me through every season."

____

____

____

____

____

Day 22 — Learning to Be Still

Key Scripture

"Be still, and know that I am God..."
— Psalm 46:10

Devotional

Being still is not always easy.

Many women carry busy minds and heavy hearts.
There is always something to think about, something to do, something to fix, or something to worry over. Even in quiet moments, the mind may still feel full.

Sometimes the body is resting, but the heart is not.

It is easy to live in a hurry.
It is easy to keep going without slowing down.
It is easy to fill every moment with noise, activity, or concern.

But God says,
"Be still, and know that I am God."

What a gentle invitation.

Being still does not mean doing nothing at all. It means quieting your heart before God. It means taking your hands off what you cannot control and remembering who He is. It means making space for His peace to settle over your soul.

Stillness is where you remember:
God is in control.
God is faithful.

God is near.
God is greater than what is troubling your heart.

Sometimes we stay restless because we feel that if we keep thinking, worrying, or striving, we will somehow hold life together better. But peace does not come from striving. Peace comes from trusting God.

When you are still before the Lord, you are not being weak.
You are making room for faith.
You are choosing to stop letting fear speak the loudest.
You are allowing the truth of God's presence to quiet your heart.

Stillness helps you hear God more clearly.

When the heart is noisy with fear, it is hard to rest.
When the mind is racing, it is hard to listen.
When the soul is restless, it is hard to feel peace.

But when you come into God's presence and become still, something beautiful happens. Your breathing slows. Your thoughts begin to settle. Your heart remembers that God is not confused. He is not absent. He is not worried about your life.

He is God.
And because He is God, you do not have to carry everything on your own.

Learning to be still may take practice. It may mean choosing prayer instead of panic. It may mean sitting quietly with Scripture. It may mean pausing in the middle of a hard day and saying, **"Lord, help my heart be still before You."**

Stillness is not just silence around you. It is peace within you.

Today, if your heart feels restless, come back to this truth:
You do not have to rush.
You do not have to strive.
You do not have to let worry rule your thoughts.

Be still.
God is with you.
God is over every detail.
God is worthy of your trust.

And in His presence, your soul can rest.

Prayer

Heavenly Father,

Thank You for inviting me to be still and know that You are God. Thank You that I do not have to live with a restless heart and an anxious mind. Thank You that in Your presence, I can find peace for my soul.

Lord, today I bring You all the noise inside of me. I bring You my worries, my rushing thoughts, my concerns, and the things that have been making my heart feel unsettled. Please quiet me in Your presence.

Teach me how to be still before You. Help me to stop striving over things I cannot control. Help me to stop letting worry lead my thoughts. Fill my heart with the peace that only You can give.

When my mind feels busy, remind me that You are God. When my heart feels troubled, remind me that You are near. When I am tempted to rush ahead in fear, help me slow down and trust You.

Father, let Your presence calm me. Let Your truth steady me. Let Your peace settle deep inside my soul. Today I choose stillness over striving. Today I choose trust over worry. Today I rest in the truth that You are God.

In Jesus' name,
Amen.

Reflection Questions

1. What usually makes your heart feel restless or unsettled?
2. Is it hard for you to slow down and be still before God?
3. What does being still and knowing that He is God mean to you personally?
4. What can you do today to make space for stillness in God's presence?

Declaration

I will be still and know that He is God.
I do not have to strive or live in worry.
God is in control, and He is near to me.
His peace will calm my heart and steady my soul.
I am a daughter of the King.

Journal Prompt

Write about what has been making your heart feel restless. Then write this truth over your soul today:
"I choose to be still before God and trust Him with every part of my life."

____

____

____

____

Day 23 — Praying Through the Storm

Key Scripture

"And he arose, and rebuked the wind, and said unto the sea, Peace, be still…"
— Mark 4:39

Devotional

Storms come in many forms.

Some storms are sudden.
Some storms last a long time.
Some storms shake your emotions, your peace, your family, your health, your faith, or your future.

A storm may be a hard season.
A painful loss.
A fearful situation.
A deep burden that will not go away quickly.

When storms come, it is easy to feel overwhelmed. It is easy to feel afraid. It is easy to wonder how long the winds will keep blowing and when peace will come again.

But one of the most powerful things a woman can do in the middle of a storm is pray.

Prayer does not always remove the storm right away.

But prayer keeps your heart connected to the One who rules over it.

In Mark 4, the wind was strong and the waves were fierce, but Jesus was still in the boat. That is such a beautiful reminder for us. Even when the storm is loud, Jesus is still present. Even when fear rises, He has not left. Even when things feel out of control, He is still Lord over the wind and the waves.

Sometimes storms make you feel powerless. They make you feel like everything is shaking around you. But prayer brings you back to truth. It reminds you that God is greater than the storm. It reminds you that you are not facing this alone.

Prayer says,
"Father, I am afraid, but I trust You."
"Lord, this is hard, but I will come to You."
"Jesus, the storm is real, but so is Your power."

That is what it means to pray through the storm.

You may cry while you pray.
You may not have many words.
You may only be able to whisper the name of Jesus.
But even that is enough to bring your heart to the Father.

Prayer in the storm is not about perfect words.
It is about staying close to God in the middle of what is hard.

Some storms will pass quickly.
Some storms will take time.
But no storm is greater than the presence of God.

He knows the waves that have been crashing against your heart.
He knows the fear that has tried to rise in your mind.
He knows the exhaustion that comes from trying to stay strong in a hard season.

And still, He says,
"Peace, be still."

Maybe today the storm around you has not calmed yet. But God can
still bring peace within you. He can steady your heart while the winds
are still blowing. He can hold you while the waves are still rising. He
can remind you that the storm is not the end of your story.

Today, do not stop praying just because the storm is loud.
Pray through the tears.
Pray through the fear.
Pray through the waiting.
Pray through the questions.

Jesus is still in the boat.
He is still near.
He is still able to speak peace over your life.

Prayer

Heavenly Father,

Thank You that I do not face storms alone. Thank You that even when
life feels heavy, uncertain, and overwhelming, You are still with me.
Thank You that no storm is greater than Your power and no burden is
beyond Your care.

Lord, today I bring You the storm I am walking through. You know
what has shaken my heart. You know the fears, the worries, the pain,
and the uncertainty I have been carrying. Please meet me in this storm.

Calm what is restless inside of me. Speak peace to my heart. When
fear rises, remind me that You are near. When I feel weak, help me
keep praying. When I do not know what to say, hear the cry of my
heart.

Father, I ask You to strengthen me in this season. Hold me steady when life feels unstable. Help me trust You when I do not understand what is happening. Remind me that You are still Lord over every wind and every wave.

Today I choose to pray through this storm. I choose to stay close to You. I choose to believe that You are with me and that Your peace can guard my heart.

In Jesus' name,
Amen.

Reflection Questions

1. What storm are you walking through right now?
2. How has this storm affected your peace, thoughts, or faith?
3. Why do you think prayer is so important in hard seasons?
4. What would it look like for you to keep praying through this storm today?

Declaration

I will pray through the storm.
Jesus is with me, even in the middle of the waves.
God is greater than what is shaking my life.
He can speak peace to my
heart. I am a daughter of the
King.

Journal Prompt

Write honestly about the storm you are facing right now. Then write this truth over your heart:
"Jesus is with me in this storm, and He will speak peace over my life."

Day 24 — When God Says Wait

Key Scripture

"Wait on the Lord: be of good courage, and he shall strengthen thine heart…"
— Psalm 27:14

Devotional

Waiting can be very hard.

It is hard when you are praying and do not see the answer yet.
It is hard when your heart is ready to move, but God is telling you to stay still.
It is hard when you do not understand why the door has not opened, why the healing has not come, or why the answer is taking so long.

Sometimes God says yes.
Sometimes God says no.
And sometimes God says wait.

That waiting place can test your heart.

It can bring impatience.
It can bring questions.
It can bring discouragement.
It can make you wonder if God has forgotten you.

But when God says wait, it is not because He does not care.
It is not because He is ignoring your prayers.
It is not because He has stopped working.

It is because His timing is perfect.

The Bible says, **"Wait on the Lord: be of good courage, and he shall strengthen thine heart."** That is such a comforting promise. God knows that waiting can be hard on the heart, so He promises to strengthen you while you wait.

He does not leave you empty in the waiting.
He gives grace in the waiting.
He gives strength in the waiting.
He gives peace in the waiting.

Sometimes what you are asking for is good, but it is not yet time.
Sometimes God is protecting you.
Sometimes He is preparing you.
Sometimes He is working in ways you cannot see.

What feels like delay to you is not delay to God.
He sees the full picture.
He knows what is ahead.
He knows the right time for every answer.

When God says wait, He is asking you to trust His heart even when you do not understand His timing.

That kind of trust takes courage.

It takes courage to keep praying.
It takes courage to keep believing.
It takes courage to stay faithful when your answer has not come yet.

But you are not waiting alone.

God is with you in the waiting room.
He is with you in the quiet season.
He is with you in the unanswered place.

And while you wait, He is strengthening your heart.

Do not believe the lie that nothing is happening.
God is always working.
Do not believe the lie that waiting means abandonment.
God is always near.
Do not believe the lie that your waiting is wasted. In God's hands, it never is.

Today, if God is asking you to wait, do not lose heart.
Let Him steady you.
Let Him strengthen you.
Let Him remind you that what He has for you will come in the right time.

When God says wait, you can still trust Him.
His timing is loving.
His wisdom is perfect.
His heart is faithful.

Prayer

Heavenly Father,

Thank You that even when You ask me to wait, You are still good and faithful. Thank You that Your timing is perfect, even when I do not understand it. Thank You that You do not leave me alone in seasons of waiting.

Lord, You know the answers I have been longing for. You know the prayers I have carried, the hopes in my heart, and the places where waiting has made me feel tired and discouraged. Sometimes it is hard for me to wait. Sometimes I want answers now. Sometimes I do not understand why things are taking so long.

Please strengthen my heart while I wait. Give me courage to trust You. Help me not to grow bitter, fearful, or impatient. Remind me that

waiting does not mean You have forgotten me. Remind me that You
are still working, even when I cannot see it.

Teach me to rest in Your timing. Teach me to trust Your wisdom more
than my own understanding. Fill my heart with peace while I wait for
Your answer. Help me stay faithful, hopeful, and close to You in this
season.

Today I choose to wait on You. Today I choose to trust Your timing.
Today I believe that You will strengthen my heart and lead me in the
right way.

In Jesus' name,
Amen.

Reflection Questions

1. What area of your life feels like a waiting place right now?
2. How has waiting affected your heart and your faith?
3. Why do you think waiting requires courage?
4. What would it look like for you to trust God's timing more
    fully today?

Declaration

I will wait on the Lord with courage.
He will strengthen my heart.
God's timing is perfect, and His heart is faithful.
My waiting is not wasted in His
hands. I am a daughter of the King.

Journal Prompt

Write about an area where God is asking you to wait. Be honest about what feels hard. Then write this truth over your heart:
"I will wait on the Lord, and He will strengthen my heart."

____

____

____

____

____

Day 25 — Clothed in Strength and Grace

Key Scripture

"Strength and honour are her clothing; and she shall rejoice in time to come."
— Proverbs 31:25

Devotional

A woman of God is not clothed only in what people can see on the outside.

Her true beauty is deeper than appearance.
It is deeper than style.
It is deeper than what the world calls success.

The Bible says, **"Strength and honour are her clothing."** What a beautiful picture. It shows a woman whose life is covered with something precious from God. She is clothed in strength and grace.

This does not mean she never feels weak.
It does not mean she never cries.
It does not mean she never walks through hard days.

It means that even in weakness, God gives her strength.
Even in pain, God teaches her grace.
Even in difficulty, God is shaping something beautiful in her life.

Strength and grace are both important.

Strength helps you stand when life is hard.
Grace helps you stay tender when life could make you hard.
Strength helps you keep going.
Grace helps you keep your heart soft before God.

A daughter of the King needs both.

Some women are strong, but they have become tired and hardened.
Some women are gentle, but they feel too weak to keep standing. But
God knows how to clothe His daughters with both strength and grace
together.

He can make you strong without making you hard.
He can make you gentle without making you weak.

That is the beauty of a woman who walks with God.

Strength and grace do not come from trying harder in your own power.
They come from staying close to the Lord. As you spend time in His
presence, He shapes your heart. He gives courage for what you face.
He gives peace for what you carry. He gives kindness for the moments
that test you.

Some days you may not feel strong.
Some days you may feel tired, stretched, or overwhelmed.
But your strength is not measured only by your feelings.

Your strength comes from God.

And His grace covers you too.

Grace reminds you that you do not have to be perfect.
Grace reminds you that God is patient with you.
Grace reminds you that even while you are growing, you are still
deeply loved.

Today, let this truth settle in your heart:

You are clothed in strength because God is with you.
You are clothed in grace because God is for you.

You do not have to fear the future when your life is in His hands.
You do not have to be shaken by every hard moment.
The God who holds you is the same God who clothes you with what
you need.

Today, walk as a daughter of the King.
Walk in His strength.
Walk in His grace.
Walk with quiet confidence, knowing that what God places on your
life is more beautiful than anything the world can offer.

Prayer

Heavenly Father,

Thank You for clothing me with strength and grace. Thank You that I
do not have to depend only on myself. Thank You that when I feel
weak, You are my strength, and when I feel tired, Your grace covers
me.

Lord, teach me to walk as a daughter of the King. Help me to carry
strength without becoming hard. Help me to carry grace without
feeling weak. Shape my heart to reflect Your beauty, Your peace, and
Your love.

When life feels heavy, strengthen me. When my heart feels stretched,
steady me. When I am tempted to become discouraged, remind me
that You are with me and that You will give me what I need for each
day.

Father, clothe me with quiet confidence in You. Let my life reflect
strength that comes from Your presence and grace that comes from

Your heart. Help me to trust You with my future and to walk in peace, knowing that my life is safe in Your hands.

Today I choose to receive Your strength. Today I choose to rest in Your grace. Today I choose to walk as Your daughter, clothed in what only You can give.

In Jesus' name,
Amen.

Reflection Questions

1. What does it mean to you to be clothed in strength and grace?
2. In what area of your life do you need God's strength right now?
3. In what area of your life do you need more grace right now?
4. How can you walk today with quiet confidence as a daughter of the King?

Declaration

I am clothed in strength and grace.
God is my strength when I feel weak.
His grace covers me each day.
I will walk with peace, dignity, and confidence in Him.
I am a daughter of the King.

Journal Prompt

Write about an area where you need God to clothe you with strength and grace today. Then write this truth over your heart:
"The Lord has clothed me with strength and grace, and I will walk in His peace."

Day 26 — A Heart Set Apart

Key Scripture

"And be not conformed to this world: but be ye transformed by the renewing of your mind..." — Romans 12:2

Devotional

A heart set apart for God does not look like the world.

It does not follow every trend.
It does not agree with everything around it.
It does not chase what the world says is important.

A heart set apart belongs to God.

This kind of heart wants to please Him.
It wants to walk in truth.
It wants to stay close to His presence.
It wants to live in a way that honors Him.

That does not mean a woman with a heart set apart is perfect.
It does not mean she never struggles. It does not mean she has no battles.

It means her heart belongs to the Lord, and she keeps turning back to Him.

The Bible says, **"Be not conformed to this world: but be ye transformed by the renewing of your mind."** The world will always try to shape the way you think, speak, live, and choose. It will tell you

to follow your feelings, lower your standards, and blend in so no one
will notice the difference.

But God calls His daughters to something higher.

He calls you to be transformed.
He calls you to think differently.
He calls you to live differently.
He calls you to love what is true, pure, and pleasing to Him.

Sometimes having a heart set apart means you will not fit in
everywhere.
Sometimes it means people may not understand your choices.
Sometimes it means walking away from things that do not honor
God, even when others think it is fine.

That can be lonely at times. But it is also beautiful.

There is peace in belonging fully to God.
There is safety in walking in His ways.
There is joy in knowing your life is pleasing to Him.

A heart set apart does not mean your life is full of rules without love.
It means your heart has been touched by God, and because of that, you
want to live close to Him. You want your thoughts to be clean. You
want your words to carry grace. You want your choices to reflect His
truth.

God is not asking you to be like everyone else. He is asking you to
be His.

That is a holy calling.

When your heart is set apart for God, you begin to care more about
His approval than the approval of people. You begin to want what He
wants. You begin to guard the things you let into your heart and mind.
You begin to love righteousness more than compromise.

This kind of life does not come by human effort alone. It comes by staying near to God. As He renews your mind, He also transforms your heart. He gives you strength to say no to what pulls you away and grace to keep walking with Him.

Today, let this be your desire:
Lord, set my heart apart for You.

Let your heart be fully His.
Let your thoughts be shaped by His Word.
Let your choices reflect His truth.
Let your life shine with quiet holiness and love.

You are a daughter of the King, and your heart was made to belong to Him.

Prayer

Heavenly Father,

Thank You for calling me to belong to You. Thank You that You have set me apart as Your daughter. Thank You that I do not have to follow the ways of this world, because You are teaching me a better way.

Lord, set my heart apart for You. Renew my mind with Your truth. Help me not to be shaped by the world around me, but by Your Word and Your presence. Teach me to love what is pleasing to You and to walk in a way that honors You.

Give me strength when I feel pressure to fit in. Give me courage when I need to stand for what is right. Help me to care more about Your approval than the approval of people. Guard my heart, my thoughts, my words, and my choices.

Father, I do not want a divided heart. I want a heart that is fully Yours. Cleanse what needs to be cleansed. Change what needs to be changed.

Draw me closer to You and help me walk in holiness, truth, and love.

Today I surrender my heart again to You. Today I ask You to set me apart for Your glory. Today I choose to belong fully to You.

In Jesus' name,
Amen.

Reflection Questions

1. What does it mean to you personally to have a heart set apart for God?
2. Are there areas in your life where you feel pressure to conform to the world?
3. How can renewing your mind with God's Word help you live differently?
4. What is one area where you want your heart to belong more fully to God?

Declaration

My heart is set apart for God.
I will not be conformed to this world.
God is renewing my mind and transforming my life.
I belong to Him, and I want to honor
Him. I am a daughter of the King.

Journal Prompt

Write about any area where you feel God calling you to live differently or more closely with Him. Then write this truth over your heart: **"Lord, my heart belongs to You, and I want to be set apart for Your glory."**

Day 27 — Living with Bold Faith

Key Scripture

"The righteous are bold as a lion." — Proverbs 28:1

Devotional

Bold faith does not mean you never feel afraid.

It does not mean you always feel strong.
It does not mean you have all the answers. It does not mean life is always easy.

Bold faith means you choose to trust God even when fear tries to speak.

Many women think bold faith looks loud, powerful, and fearless all the time. But sometimes bold faith is quiet. Sometimes it looks like praying when you feel weak. Sometimes it looks like standing on God's Word when your emotions are shaking. Sometimes it looks like taking one small step of obedience when you are unsure of the outcome.

That is still bold faith.

The Bible says, **"The righteous are bold as a lion."** This kind of boldness does not come from human pride. It comes from knowing who God is and knowing who you are in Him. When your heart is anchored in the Lord, you can stand with courage because your confidence is not in yourself. Your confidence is in God.

Bold faith says,
"God is with me."
"God will help me."
"God is greater than what I face."

A daughter of the King does not have to live small because of fear. She does not have to stay silent because of insecurity. She does not have to shrink back when God is calling her to trust Him, speak truth, pray, serve, or keep moving forward.

Fear says,
"Stay back."

Bold faith says,
"God is with me, so I will go forward."

There may be moments when your heart trembles. There may be times when you wonder if you are strong enough. But remember this: bold faith is not trusting in your own strength. It is trusting in the strength of the Lord.

God can make you brave in places where you once felt weak. He can give you courage to speak when you once stayed silent. He can help you stand when you once wanted to hide.

Living with bold faith may mean: trusting God with your future, obeying Him when it is uncomfortable, praying with confidence, speaking truth with love, or refusing to let fear control your life.

You do not have to wait until you feel completely ready.

Sometimes faith grows as you step forward.

God does not ask you to be bold by yourself. He gives you His Spirit, His Word, His presence, and His strength. The same God who calls you forward will help you stand.

Today, do not let fear decide your steps.
Do not let insecurity silence your faith.
Do not let the enemy convince you to live smaller than God has called you to live.

You are a daughter of the King.
You are not without help.
You are not without strength.
You are not without purpose.

Walk forward with bold faith.
Not because you feel strong in yourself, but because your God is faithful, mighty, and near.

Prayer

Heavenly Father,

Thank You that I do not have to live ruled by fear. Thank You that You are with me and that my confidence can be in You. Thank You that bold faith does not come from my own strength, but from Your presence and power in my life.

Lord, today I ask You to fill me with courage. In every area where fear has held me back, help me trust You more. In every place where insecurity has made me feel small, remind me who I am in You. In every place where I have been tempted to shrink back, give me grace to stand and move forward in faith.

Teach me to live with bold faith. Help me pray boldly, trust boldly, obey boldly, and walk boldly in the calling You have for my life. Let my heart be anchored in Your truth and not in my feelings. Let my confidence come from knowing that You are with me.

Father, I surrender my fears to You. I surrender my hesitation, my doubts, and the places where I feel weak. Fill those places with Your strength. Help me not to be controlled by fear, but led by faith.

Today I choose to trust You. Today I choose to step forward in courage.
Today I believe that because You are with me, I can live with bold faith.

In Jesus' name,
Amen.

Reflection Questions

1. Are there areas in your life where fear has been holding you back?
2. What does living with bold faith mean to you personally?
3. Is God calling you to step forward in any area right now?
4. How can you choose faith over fear today?

Declaration

I will live with bold faith.
My confidence is in the Lord.
I will not be ruled by fear.
God is with me, and He will help me stand.
I am a daughter of the King.

Journal Prompt

Write about an area where you feel God calling you to be brave and trust Him more. Then write this truth over your heart:
"Because God is with me, I can walk forward with bold faith."

Day 28 — Serving with Love

Key Scripture

"By love serve one another." — Galatians 5:13

Devotional

Serving is a beautiful part of the Christian life.

When your heart belongs to God, love begins to flow outward. You begin to care for others, pray for others, encourage others, and help where you can. Serving is one way the love of God is seen through your life.

But true service is not only about what you do. It is also about the spirit in which you do it.

The Bible says, **"By love serve one another."** That means love should be the reason behind your service. Not pride. Not pressure. Not trying to impress people. Not trying to earn value. But love.

A daughter of the King serves because she has been loved by God.
She gives because she has received grace.
She cares because the heart of Jesus is growing in her.

Serving with love may look different in different seasons.

Sometimes it looks like helping someone in a practical way.
Sometimes it looks like listening to a hurting heart.
Sometimes it looks like praying for someone quietly.
Sometimes it looks like giving encouragement, kindness, or time.

Not every act of service is seen by many people.
Some of the most beautiful acts of love happen in quiet places.

God sees them all.

He sees the kindness no one else noticed.
He sees the prayer you whispered for someone.
He sees the help you offered when you were tired.
He sees the love you gave without asking for attention.

Serving with love also means serving with the right heart. It is possible
to do good things but still become tired, resentful, or empty inside.
That is why your heart must stay connected to God. You cannot pour
out well if you are not first receiving from Him.

You are not called to serve from pressure.
You are called to serve from love.

That is a big difference.

When love leads your service, there is beauty in it. There is humility in
it. There is peace in it. It becomes an offering to the Lord, not just an
action in front of people.

Jesus Himself is our example. He served with humility, compassion,
and love. He did not serve to be praised. He served because love was
at the center of His heart.

As His daughter, you are called to reflect that same spirit.

Today, let your service flow from love, not from striving.
Let your kindness be sincere.
Let your helping hands be guided by grace.
Let your heart stay soft and humble before the Lord.

And remember this too:

Serving with love does not mean saying yes to everything. It means being led by God in how you give, how you care, and how you serve. Love is not forced. Love is faithful, gentle, and wise.

Today ask yourself:
How can I reflect the love of Jesus to someone today?

It may be through a word.
A prayer.
A smile.
A small act of
kindness.
A quiet sacrifice.

Whatever it is, let it be done in love.

Because when a daughter of the King serves with love, she reflects the heart of her Father.

Prayer

Heavenly Father,

Thank You for loving me so deeply. Thank You for serving me with grace, mercy, and kindness every day. Thank You that because I have received Your love, I can now give love to others.

Lord, teach me to serve with the right heart. Help me not to serve from pressure, pride, or the need for approval. Help me serve from love. Let my actions reflect the heart of Jesus. Let my words carry kindness. Let my hands be willing to help where You lead me.

Father, keep my heart humble and soft. Guard me from resentment, weariness, and striving. Help me stay close to You so that I can give from a place of love and not emptiness. Fill me again with Your grace so that what flows out of me will be sincere and pleasing to You.

Show me how to love others well today. Give me wisdom in how to serve, when to speak, when to help, and how to reflect Your compassion. Let my life be an offering of love to You.

Today I choose to serve with love. Today I choose to reflect the heart of Jesus. Today I ask You to make my life a blessing to others for Your glory.

In Jesus' name,
Amen.

Reflection Questions

1. What does serving with love mean to you personally?
2. Have there been times when you served from pressure instead of from love?
3. How can staying close to God help you serve others with the right heart?
4. Who might God be leading you to love or encourage today?

Declaration

I will serve with love.
I have received God's love, and I will share it with others.
My service will flow from grace, humility, and kindness.
I want my life to reflect the heart of Jesus.
I am a daughter of the King.

Journal Prompt

Write about an area where God is teaching you to serve with love.
Then write this truth over your heart:
"Lord, let my life reflect Your love in the way I serve others."

____

____

____

____

____

Day 29 — Speaking Life

Key Scripture

"Death and life are in the power of the tongue..." — Proverbs 18:21

Devotional

Words are powerful.

They can heal or hurt.
They can build up or tear down.
They can bring peace or bring pain.

Many women know what it feels like to carry the weight of words. Some have been deeply hurt by words spoken over them. Some have believed harsh things said in anger, rejection, or carelessness. Words can leave marks on the heart for a long time.

But words can also bring life.

The Bible says, **"Death and life are in the power of the tongue."** That means what we say matters. Our words are not small. They carry influence. They can strengthen a heart, comfort a soul, encourage faith, and reflect the love of God.

A daughter of the King is called to speak life.

That does not mean she is never honest.
It does not mean she pretends everything is perfect.
It does not mean she never corrects or speaks truth.

It means her words are guided by wisdom, love, and grace.

Speaking life means choosing words that heal instead of wound.
It means speaking hope instead of constant fear.
It means speaking kindness instead of bitterness.
It means speaking truth without cruelty.

This also includes the words you speak to yourself.

Sometimes the harshest words a woman hears are the ones she says in her own heart:
I am not enough.
I always fail.
Nothing will ever change.
I will never get through this.

But those are not words of life.

God wants to teach you to speak differently. He wants your mouth and your heart to agree with His truth. He wants your words to reflect faith more than fear. He wants your speech to become a place where grace lives.

Speaking life may look like: encouraging someone who is weary, praying over your family, blessing instead of cursing, speaking truth over your own heart, or choosing silence when angry words want to rise.

A woman who speaks life does not use her mouth to destroy what God is trying to heal. She learns to let the Holy Spirit guide her words. She asks, **"Lord, let my words be pleasing to You."**

Not every thought should be spoken.
Not every hurt feeling should become harmful speech.
Not every moment of anger should control your tongue.

God can help you speak with wisdom.

When His love fills your heart, life begins to come out of your mouth.
When His peace fills your soul, gentleness begins to shape your
words. When His truth renews your mind, your speech begins to carry
light.

Today, remember this:
Your words matter.
They matter in your home.
They matter in your friendships.
They matter in ministry.
They matter in the way you speak to yourself.

Ask God to make your mouth a place of life.

Let your words comfort.
Let your words bless.
Let your words heal.
Let your words reflect the heart of Jesus.

Because when a daughter of the King speaks life, she carries the
beauty of heaven into the lives of others.

Prayer

Heavenly Father,

Thank You for reminding me that my words matter. Thank You that
You can teach me to speak with wisdom, grace, and love. Thank You
that You are able to heal not only my heart, but also the way I speak.

Lord, forgive me for the times my words have not reflected Your heart.
Forgive me for harsh words, fearful words, negative words, or careless
words. Forgive me for the times I have spoken against myself instead
of agreeing with Your truth.

Please guard my mouth and guide my words. Let my speech bring life, peace, and encouragement. Help me speak with kindness when I am hurt, with wisdom when I am upset, and with grace when I am tired. Teach me to pause before I speak and to let Your Spirit shape what comes out of my mouth.

Father, also heal the words I speak over my own heart. Remove every lie, every harsh judgment, and every hopeless thought. Help me speak truth over myself according to Your Word. Let my mouth agree with what You say about me.

Today I choose to speak life. Today I choose to let my words be filled with grace. Today I ask You to make my mouth an instrument of healing, truth, and love.

In Jesus' name,
Amen.

Reflection Questions

1. Have words ever deeply hurt you?
2. How do you usually speak when you are tired, stressed, or upset?
3. Are there negative words you have been speaking over yourself?
4. What would it look like for you to speak more life-giving words today?

Declaration

I will speak life with my words.
My mouth will reflect wisdom, grace, and love.
I will not agree with fear, bitterness, or lies.
God will help me speak words that heal and bless.
I am a daughter of the King.

Journal Prompt

Write about the kind of words you want to speak more often in your life.
Then write this truth over your heart:
"Lord, let my words bring life, healing, and grace."

Day 30 — Walking in Purpose

Key Scripture

"For we are his workmanship, created in Christ Jesus unto good works, which God hath before ordained that we should walk in them."
— Ephesians 2:10

Devotional

Every woman wants to know that her life matters.

Deep in the heart, there is often a question:
Why am I here?
What is God's plan for my life?
Does my life truly have purpose?

The answer is yes.

Your life has purpose because God made you on purpose.

The Bible says, **"For we are his workmanship, created in Christ Jesus unto good works..."** That means you are not an accident. You are not here by chance. God formed you with care, and He has meaning for your life.

Purpose is not only about big things that people can see.
It is not only about titles, platforms, or public work.
Sometimes people think purpose must look great in the eyes of others.
But in God's Kingdom, purpose often begins in quiet places.

Purpose may look like: loving your family well, praying faithfully, encouraging someone who is hurting, serving in small ways, walking in obedience, sharing your testimony, or being a light where God has placed you.

A woman walking in purpose does not have to compare her path with someone else's. God has not asked you to live someone else's calling. He has asked you to walk faithfully in the life He has given you.

Comparison can make purpose feel far away.
Fear can make purpose feel too big.
Pain can make purpose feel hidden.
But God is still able to lead you.

Sometimes purpose unfolds little by little.
Sometimes it becomes clearer as you obey one step at a time.
Sometimes it grows through the very things you have walked through.

The pain you endured may become part of the comfort you offer others. The lessons you learned may become part of your testimony. The doors God opens may reveal new ways to serve, love, and reflect Him.

Walking in purpose does not mean you have every answer about your future. It means you are willing to walk with God today.

Purpose begins with relationship.
As you stay close to God, He guides your steps.
As you obey Him, He shapes your path. As you trust Him, He shows you more.

A daughter of the King does not have to panic about finding purpose. She can rest in the truth that the One who created her also knows how to lead her. He is not confused about her life. He is not late in revealing what she needs to know. He is faithful to direct her.

Today, do not believe the lie that your life is small or without meaning.

Do not believe the lie that your best days are behind you. Do not believe the lie that God has no plan for you.

You are His workmanship.
You are created with purpose.
You are called to walk with Him.

Even if your next step seems simple, it still matters.
Even if your calling feels quiet, it is still precious to God.
Even if you are still growing, God is still working.

Walk in purpose today by saying yes to God in the place where you are.

Prayer

Heavenly Father,

Thank You that my life has purpose because You created me. Thank You that I am not an accident and that You formed me with care, love, and intention. Thank You that You have prepared good works for me and that You know exactly how to lead me.

Lord, help me walk in purpose. Remove every lie that tells me my life does not matter. Remove every fear that makes me shrink back. Remove every comparison that steals my peace. Help me trust the path You have for me.

Teach me to walk faithfully in the place where I am right now. Open my eyes to the ways I can serve, love, obey, and reflect You. Show me the good works You have placed before me. Help me not to overlook the small things, because I know they matter to You.

Father, I do not want to chase purpose in my own way. I want to walk closely with You and let You guide my life. Shape my heart, direct my steps, and use my life for Your glory. Let my story, my words, my prayers, and my obedience become part of Your beautiful plan.

Today I choose to trust that my life has purpose. Today I choose to walk with You one step at a time. Today I believe that You are leading me in the path You have prepared for me.

In Jesus' name,
Amen.

Reflection Questions

1. Have you ever struggled to believe that your life has purpose?
2. In what ways has comparison or fear affected how you see your calling?
3. What does it mean to you that you are God's workmanship?
4. What is one simple way you can walk in purpose today?

Declaration

My life has purpose because God created me.
I am His workmanship.
I do not have to compare my path to anyone else's.
God is leading me, and I will walk faithfully with
Him. I am a daughter of the King.

Journal Prompt

Write about the areas where you desire more clarity about your purpose.
Then write this truth over your heart:
"God created me with purpose, and He will guide me as I walk with Him."

____

____

____

____

____

Day 31 — Crowned with Peace

Key Scripture

"And the peace of God, which passeth all understanding, shall keep your hearts and minds through Christ Jesus." — Philippians 4:7

Devotional

Peace is one of the most precious gifts God gives to His daughters.

This peace is not like the peace the world offers.
Worldly peace depends on circumstances.
It depends on everything going well.
It depends on answers, comfort, and things feeling under control.

But the peace of God is different.

It can remain even when life feels uncertain.
It can stay even when questions are still unanswered.
It can hold your heart even when the road ahead is not fully clear.

That is why the Bible says, **"The peace of God, which passeth all understanding, shall keep your hearts and minds through Christ Jesus."** This is a peace that goes beyond human explanation. It is peace that comes from the presence of God.

Many women long for peace.

They want peace in their mind.
Peace in their emotions.

Peace in their home.
Peace in the middle of hard seasons, difficult relationships, and personal battles.

And God delights to give peace to the heart that trusts Him.

Being crowned with peace does not mean you never face trouble. It does not mean there are no more tears, no more waiting, or no more trials.

It means that in the middle of it all, God places His peace over you like a covering.

What a beautiful picture.

You are crowned, not with fear.
You are crowned, not with confusion.
You are crowned, not with heaviness.
You are crowned with peace.

This peace guards your heart when anxiety tries to enter. It guards your mind when fearful thoughts try to take over. It steadies your soul when life feels unsettled.

Peace does not come from having every answer.
Peace comes from knowing the One who holds every answer.

When you stay close to Jesus, His peace begins to settle over your life. It does not always mean you understand everything. But it means your heart can rest in the One who does.

Sometimes women live as if peace is something far away. They think:
I will have peace when this changes.
I will have peace when this problem is over.
I will have peace when I finally know what will happen.

But God's peace is not only for later.
It is for now.

Right here in the middle of the unknown, right here in the middle of
the healing journey, right here in the middle of the waiting season,
God can still crown you with peace.

This peace is part of your inheritance as His daughter.

You do not have to live ruled by worry.
You do not have to let fear sit on the throne of your thoughts.
You do not have to carry inner turmoil every day.

You can come to the Father.
You can place every care before Him.
You can ask Him to guard your heart and mind with His peace.

And He will.

Today, let this truth settle deeply into your soul:
The peace of God belongs to you in Christ.
He can calm what feels restless.
He can quiet what feels anxious.
He can steady what feels shaken.

As this 31-day journey comes to a close, remember this:
You are chosen.
You are loved.
You are healed.
You are strengthened.
You are guided.
You are not alone.

And now, as a daughter of the King, you are crowned with peace.

Walk forward with that peace.
Rest in that peace.
Guard your heart with that peace.
And trust that the God who began a good work in you will continue to
lead you in grace, love, and faithfulness.

Prayer

Heavenly Father,

Thank You for the gift of Your peace. Thank You that Your peace is greater than my understanding and stronger than my fears. Thank You that even when life feels uncertain, I can rest in You.

Lord, today I ask You to crown me with peace. Guard my heart from anxiety. Guard my mind from fearful thoughts. Calm every place in me that feels restless, troubled, or overwhelmed. Let Your peace rule in my heart.

Teach me to bring every burden to You. Teach me to trust You with the things I cannot control. When questions rise, remind me that You are still faithful. When fear tries to speak, remind me that Your peace is greater. When life feels heavy, cover me with Your calm and steady presence.

Father, thank You for carrying me through every part of this journey. Thank You for reminding me who I am in You. Thank You for healing, strengthening, and teaching me day by day. Help me walk forward from this place with a peaceful heart, a renewed mind, and deeper trust in You.

Today I receive Your peace. Today I choose to rest in Your presence. Today I declare that through Christ, my heart and mind are kept by the peace of God.

In Jesus' name,
Amen.

Reflection Questions

1. What usually tries to steal your peace?
2. In what area of your life do you need God's peace the most right now?

3. What does it mean to you that God's peace can guard your heart and mind?
4. How can you walk forward in greater peace each day?

Declaration

I am crowned with peace.
The peace of God guards my heart and mind.
I do not have to live ruled by fear or anxiety.
I rest in the faithful presence of my Heavenly
Father. I am a daughter of the King.

Journal Prompt

Write about the areas where you need God's peace most right now.
Then write this truth over your heart:
"The peace of God guards my heart and mind, and I am crowned with peace."

____

____

____

____

____

A Closing Word

Dear sister,

You have now come to the end of this 31-day journey.

But this is not the end of God's work in your life.

The same God who has walked with you through these pages will continue to walk with you every day ahead. The same God who has comforted you, strengthened you, corrected you, and loved you here will remain faithful in every season to come.

As you close this book, remember what God has been speaking over your heart:

You are chosen.
You are deeply loved.
You are accepted in His presence.
You are not an orphan.
You are being healed.
You are being strengthened.
You are being led.
You are clothed in grace.
You are walking in purpose.
You are crowned with peace.

You may still have questions.
You may still be growing.
You may still be healing in some places.

And that is okay.

God is patient with you.
God is near to you.
God is not finished with you.

Keep seeking Him.
Keep praying.
Keep trusting.
Keep walking one day at a time with your Heavenly Father.

When fear tries to return, remember His truth.
When sorrow feels heavy, remember His comfort.
When life feels uncertain, remember His faithfulness.
When your heart grows tired, remember His strength.
When you feel forgotten, remember you belong to Him.

You are a daughter of the King.

Walk forward with your head lifted, not in pride, but in peace. Walk
forward knowing that the Lord is with you. Walk forward knowing
that His hand is upon your life. Walk forward knowing that your story
is still being written by a faithful God.

May your heart remain close to Him.
May your mind be filled with His truth.
May your steps be guided by His wisdom.
May your life reflect His beauty.
May His peace guard you.
May His grace sustain you.
May His love carry you.

And may you always remember:

You are not alone.
You are not forgotten.
You are not without purpose.
You are His.

Final Blessing

May the Lord bless you and keep you.

May He draw you near to His heart.

May He heal every wounded place in you.

May He strengthen you for every season ahead.

May He fill your heart with peace and your mouth with prayer.

May He remind you daily that you are loved, chosen, and called by name.

May you walk in grace, truth, courage, and quiet confidence as a daughter of the King.

In Jesus' name,

Amen.

Author's Note

Dear beautiful sister,

Thank you for taking this journey through **Prayers of a Daughter of the King**.

It is such a blessing to share these pages with you.

This book was written from a heart that knows both pain and grace. Like many women, I have seen seasons of struggle, waiting, healing, and learning to trust God more deeply. I know what it is like to need His comfort, His strength, His peace, and His presence. And I also know that through every season, God remains faithful.

That is why this book is so precious to me.

My desire in writing it was not to offer perfect words, but to point your heart to a perfect God. I wanted these devotionals and prayers to feel like a gentle reminder that no matter what you have walked through, you are still deeply loved by your Heavenly Father. You are not forgotten. You are not alone. You are not without hope.

If some of these pages met you in a tender place, I pray they reminded you that God sees you. If some of these prayers gave words to what you were feeling, I pray they helped draw you closer to His heart. If some of these truths challenged you, I pray they also strengthened you.

This book is for the woman who is healing.
For the woman who is waiting.
For the woman who is weary.
For the woman who is praying through tears.
For the woman who needs to remember who she is in Christ.

And if that woman is you, I want to remind you again:

You are a daughter of the King.

As you continue your journey, I pray you will keep seeking God daily. Keep opening His Word. Keep praying, even when the prayers feel small. Keep trusting, even when the road feels uncertain. Keep giving Him your heart again and again. He is faithful to carry you, strengthen you, and lead you.

Thank you for allowing me to be part of your quiet time with the Lord through this book. It is an honor and a blessing.

May the Lord continue to heal your heart, renew your mind, and fill your life with His presence and peace.

With love and prayer,
Dr. Lende Click